Contents

Europeans Come to Turtle Island

Indigenous People Today

Teaching Tips

Encourage Topic Interest

Help students develop an understanding and appreciation of Indigenous Peoples of Canada concepts by providing an area in the classroom to display topic-related non-fiction books, pictures, collections, and artifacts as a springboard for learning.

What I Think I Know / What I Would Like to Know Activity

Introduce each concept by asking students what they think they know about the topic, and what they would like to know about the topic. Complete this activity as a whole-group brainstorming session, in cooperative small groups or independently. Once students have had a chance to complete the questions, combine the information to create a class chart for display. Throughout the study, periodically update students' progress in accomplishing their goal of what they want to know, and validate what they think they know.

Vocabulary List

Keep track of new and content-related vocabulary on chart paper for students' reference. Encourage students to add words to the list. In addition, have students create their own dictionaries as part of their learning logs.

Learning Logs

Keeping a learning log is an effective way for students to organize thoughts and ideas presented and examined. Students' learning logs also provide insight on what follow-up activities are needed to review, and clarify concepts learned.

Learning logs can include the following types of entries:

• Teacher prompts
• Students' personal reflections
• Questions that arise
• Connections discovered
• Labelled diagrams and pictures
• Definitions for new vocabulary

Who are the Indigenous People?

First Nations, the Inuit, and the Métis—these three groups are all Indigenous people.

First Nations

In the past, some people called the First Nations "Indians." Experts say the name was likely first used in the late 1400s, when explorer Christopher Columbus got lost while looking for India. Instead, he landed in what is today called North America. Columbus thought he was in India, so he called the people living here Indians.

Today, most First Nations don't like the name, but it is still used in some legal documents. There are more than 600 recognized First Nations across the country, each with its own art, culture, language, and music.

Inuit and Métis

The word "Inuit" means "the people." Inuit is the name for a number of these northern people—one person is an Inuk. These people of Canada's Arctic used to be called Eskimos, but today they consider that name a rude or negative term, and it is not widely used.

The name "Métis" was first used in the mid-1600s, when members of some First Nations began marrying Europeans. The Métis have their own unique culture that blends aspects of both groups. The Métis live mostly in Alberta, Saskatchewan, Manitoba, and Ontario.

Indigenous People Today

There are about 1.7 million Indigenous people living in Canada today. That's almost 5% of the country's population. About one million of these people are First Nations, almost 600,000 are Métis, and close to 100,000 are Inuit. National Indigenous Peoples Day, on June 21, celebrates all three groups. Visit this website for more information on National Indigenous Peoples Day:

http://www.aadnc-aandc.gc.ca/eng/1100100013248/1100100013249

Turtle Island

Today, most Indigenous people call North America Turtle Island. Here is one of the stories behind the name. It involves the Creator and a few very brave animals.

First Came the Floods

Long, long ago, people began arguing with each other. They disagreed about everything. Then they began battling each other. The people fought so much that they made the Creator unhappy. So he decided to cause a huge flood to cover the Earth with water and purify it. Soon, all the people were gone and only a few animals were left.

But the animals could find no land where they could live. What could they do? After much discussion, they decided to try to grab a pawful of earth from far, far below the water. The animals planned to use the earth to make new land where they could raise their families.

Many animals took turns diving down through the waters. Each held its breath and plunged deep, deep, deep down, trying to reach the bottom. But none of the animals could dive that far down.

They all knew the loon was a good diver and thought for sure he could reach the bottom. He dove as far down as he could. The animals at the surface peered into the water as they waited for the loon to come back. But when he finally returned to the surface he had no earth with him. Now what would the animals do?

The Muskrat Tries

The muskrat offered to try to dive and find some earth. The other animals all laughed at him. They knew he wasn't used to diving. But the muskrat wanted to try anyway. He took a deep, deep, deep breath and dove down through the water.

The other animals watched for the muskrat to return. They waited and they waited. But there was no sign of the muskrat. What had happened to him?

The animals were just about to give up when finally the muskrat broke the surface of the water. He was panting and gasping and so out of breath that he couldn't talk. But he held out his paw and there, clutched in his paw, was a little ball of earth. Even though all the animals had laughed at him, the muskrat was the only one that had been able to dive deep enough.

Turtle Island Is Born

The turtle offered his strong back to hold up the piece of earth. Soon the wind blew and blew on it. The breezes helped the earth grow until it formed an island. It became heavier and heavier, but still the turtle carried the island's weight on his back.

The wind continued to blow. Finally, there was a huge island in the midst of all the waters. Now the animals had a home.

Many Indigenous peoples, including the Ojibway, call the whole world Turtle Island. Since Mother Earth provides everyone with food, air, water, and shelter, it's important that people take good care of our planet and home.

Learn about other creation stories at:
https://www.historymuseum.ca/cmc/exhibitions/aborig/fp/fpz2f02e.shtml

---

"Turtle Island"–Think About It

1. What did the Creator hope to achieve by covering the Earth with water?
2. Why did the animals decide to try to grab some earth from below the water?
3. Why did the animals think the loon would be able to reach the bottom?
4. What did the muskrat have clutched in his paw when he resurfaced?
5. How did the animals finally come to have a home?
6. Do you think we should call the world Turtle Island? Why or why not? Explain your thinking.
7. Write your own creation story.

Peoples of the Northwest Coast

On the coast of British Columbia, between the Pacific Ocean and the mountains, lived the First Nations known as the Peoples of the Northwest Coast. These included groups such as the Coast Salish, Gitxsan, Haida, Nisga'a, Nuu-chah-nulth (Nootka), and Tlingit.

Large Homes and Canoes

Many First Nations moved around, following migrating animals. But the Peoples of the Northwest Coast lived in an area full of trees for building that also provided fish and other animals to eat. So these Indigenous people built permanent villages, close to fresh water.

The homes in these villages were large rectangular buildings made of wood. The homes were so big that they could fit between 30 and 60 members of an extended family.

The canoes of these First Nations were also large. They had to be, to stand up to the ocean's high waves and strong currents. These canoes could hold as many as 40 or 50 people. Some were used for fishing and some were war canoes.

Fishing and Feasting

Northwest Coast peoples were talented fishermen. The men constructed traps and nets to catch salmon, halibut, and other fish. Clams, crabs, and oysters were some of the sea creatures that the women gathered.

Peoples of the Northwest Coast mostly ate fish, but they also hunted animals such as bears, deer, water birds, and whales. As well, they ate berries, camas (wild hyacinth) bulbs, ferns, and seaweed.

Feasting was a big part of the potlatch ceremony, which is still an important event for Northwest Coast peoples. It can include several hundred people and is a time to mark births, deaths, and marriages, as well as political and spiritual events.

Potlatches might last several days and involved dancing and singing, as well as the exchange of presents, such as woven blankets or carved boxes.

Totem Poles and Masks

Peoples of the Northwest Coast are still well-known for the beautiful totem poles they carve. There are different types of these poles. Family or clan poles were carved in the shapes of animals, such as Killer Whale, Thunderbird, and Wolf.

A totem pole with a grave box at the top was a mortuary pole—in the box were the remains of an important person. When a chief died, a memorial pole was raised in his memory.

The colours used to paint the totem poles have important meanings. For instance, black is for power, while white represents the heavens. Blue is the colour of sky and water, and red symbolizes war.

Totem poles use animal and plant images to represent family, clan, and tribe.

Totem poles were often carved from cedar trees. These trees also provided wood for houses and canoes, while cedar branches were braided into fishing lines, nets, ropes, and more. Cedar bark was woven into clothing or hats.

But before the Northwest Coast peoples took any part of the cedar tree, they placed their hands on the tree and said a prayer of thanks. The people took only what they needed.

Learn about totem poles by watching this video found at:
http://www.aadnc-aandc.gc.ca/eng/1472670112251/1472670146699

"Peoples of the Northwest Coast"–Think About It

1. Name three First Nations who lived on the Northwest Coast.
2. Why did Northwest Coast peoples build permanent villages, instead of moving from place to place?
3. What else besides fish did Northwest Coast First Nations eat?
4. What is a *mortuary pole*?
5. List four colours used to paint totem poles and explain their meanings.
6. What, besides totem poles, were cedar trees used for? List three things.

Indigenous Peoples of Canada © Chalkboard Publishing Inc.

Peoples of the Plateau

The Peoples of the Plateau lived in what is today British Columbia, between the Coast Mountains and the Rocky Mountains. Ktunaxa (Kootenay), Okanagan, Secwepemc (Shuswap), and Stl'atl'imx (Lillooet) were some of the peoples who lived here. They travelled around to hunt and gather plants but in winter came back to their villages.

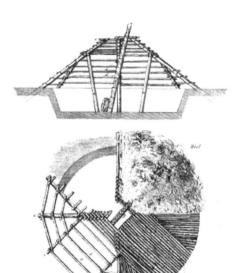

Life on the Plateau

Much of the year, Plateau peoples lived in lean-tos, lodges, or tipis. But in the winter, they stayed in pit homes that were partially underground. These looked like large domes covered with earth and tree boughs. A notched log sticking out the hole at the top of the dome helped people climb down into the home. Several families lived in each pit house.

A pit house is covered with several layers of tree boughs and sod. You enter and exit using a ladder made from a notched log.

Hunting and Preserving

The many rivers in the area teemed with salmon and the Peoples of the Plateau had many ways of catching them. They harpooned fish, standing on specific fishing rocks whose location they passed down through generations of families. Or, fishermen dipped fishing nets into the water to catch the salmon. The people also speared the fish or trapped fish in woven baskets.

To preserve the fish so it could be eaten throughout the long, cold winter, the Peoples of the Plateau dried the fish in the open air or in a smokehouse.

The Plateau First Nations also hunted, using bows and arrows, spears, and traps to catch black bears, elk, mountain goats, and other animals. Women gathered berries, lichen, nuts, roots, and more. Some were eaten right away, while others were preserved and kept for the winter.

On Land or Water

There are many rapids and fast rivers in the Plateau area, so travelling by water could be dangerous. Most of the First Nations here walked, often carrying heavy packs along the well-used trails. In winter, they loaded packs onto toboggans and trekked through the deep snow on snowshoes. Theys strapped on round "bear paw" snowshoes when carrying heavy loads, and longer, thinner snowshoes when they wanted to move faster.

On calm waters, these First Nations used rafts and bull boats. These were large, round boats made by stretching animal skin over a wood frame.

Peoples of the Plateau also used dugout canoes (carved from birch, cedar, or pine), as well as sturgeon-nosed canoes. These had pointed tips that sat just above the waterline. The unique shape helped keep water out of the canoe as it went through rapids or lakes.

In the 1730s, horses arrived in the area from the south. They made travel much faster and easier because they could carry people and packs. The Ktunaxa people were the first of the Plateau First Nations to ride horses.

Beautiful Baskets

The Stl'atl'imx peoples are one of the groups still known for the baskets they make from cedar tree roots. These tightly woven baskets are made waterproof by soaking in water. Then they can be used as cooking pots or for carrying goods. They are intricately decorated with black and red patterns.

"Peoples of the Plateau"–Think About It

1. Where did the Peoples of the Plateau live?
2. Describe a pit house.
3. What were three methods Plateau First Nations used to catch fish?
4. Name two ways Plateau First Nations travelled in winter.
5. What is a *sturgeon-nosed canoe*? What is unique about it?
6. What are the Stl'atl'imx peoples still known for?

Indigenous Peoples of Canada © Chalkboard Publishing Inc.

Peoples of the Plains

The area known today as Canada's Prairies is where the Peoples of the Plains lived—and still do. They travelled across what is now Alberta, Saskatchewan, and much of Manitoba.

Following the herds of buffalo, these First Nations moved around throughout the year. They stopped in winter only to set up their tipis in valleys that protected them from blowing winds. The Peoples of the Plains included such groups as the Assiniboine (Nakoda), Kainai (Blood), Nehiyauak (Plains Cree), Pikuni (Peigan), and Siksika (Blackfoot).

Tipi Life

The Peoples of the Plains lived in tipis, both when they were travelling and when they settled in an area. These homes were easy to transport and set up.

First, a frame of pine poles was set up in a cone shape and tied near the top. Next, buffalo hides were placed over the frame and fastened in place. Pegs and rocks kept the tipi upright, no matter how hard the winds blew.

To move a tipi, it was taken apart and the poles and hides placed on a travois. This is a frame made by fastening two pine poles together in a V-shape. A travois was pulled by a dog or, after the early 1700s, a horse. Wood was scarce on the Prairies so the pine poles were precious and carefully saved.

Bands of between 50 and 100 First Nations lived together in a settlement. Each band had about 30 or 40 tipis.

Hunters of the Buffalo

Buffalo provided the Plains people with meat, clothing, tools, and much more. The huge animals were vital to the

To carry their possessions, Peoples of the Plains used the travois. This was a V-shaped frame made of pine poles.

survival of these First Nations, so they had a number of ways of hunting the buffalo (which is also known as bison).

The hunters could guide the animals into a corral that they couldn't escape. Or the Plains people chased a herd of buffalo to a cliff, where the animals would fall over the edge. These were known as buffalo jumps, which is how Head-Smashed-In Buffalo Jump, in Alberta, got its name.

Not all the buffalo meat could be eaten at once, so some was dried. Women then pounded it into a powder and mixed it with hot fat and dried berries. Next, it was pressed into a loaf to make a long-lasting, lightweight, nutritious food for the men when they were out on the trails.

The Peoples of the Plains used buffalo hides to make clothing, and the animals' bones for tools. Buffalo tendons were used as thread, the horns as cups, and the tail as whisks.

As well as buffalo, the Peoples of the Plains also hunted elk, prairie chickens, and pronghorn antelopes. They used bows and arrows, snares, and spears to catch these animals.

Quillwork

Plains people are famous for using porcupine quills to create intricate embroidery. They added this quillwork to their animal-skin bags, clothing, and moccasins, among other items. Quills from different parts of the porcupine's body had different uses. For instance, the quills from the porcupine's tail were used for fringes and the thin quills from the belly for fine, delicate lines of embroidery.

"Peoples of the Plains"–Think About It

1. Which three provinces did the Peoples of the Plains travel across?

2. Why did the Plains First Nations move around throughout the year?

3. Give another name for each of these First Nations: Assiniboine, Kainai, Nehiyauak, Pikuni, and Siksika.

4. What is a *travois*?

5. What, besides food, did the people of the Plains use buffalo for? Name five things.

6. Which items did the Peoples of the Plains adorn with porcupine quillwork?

Indigenous Peoples of Canada © Chalkboard Publishing Inc.

Peoples of the Arctic

Another Indigenous group in Canada are the Inuit (pronounced *In-noo-it*). The Inuit were the first people to live in North America's Arctic region, arriving there about 1,000 years ago. Although "Innu" and "Inuit" sound the same, they are not related. The Inuit are a distinct people; they are not related to any other Indigenous group.

Location

Although some Inuit live in Greenland and Alaska, in Canada most live in four regions called the Inuit Nunangat. This means "the place where Inuit live." These four regions are: northern Quebec, northern Labrador, the Northwest Territories and Yukon, and Nunavut. Nunavut means "our land." Nunavut is Canada's largest and newest territory. It was formed in 1999 out of the Northwest Territories. Most of Canada's Inuit live in Nunavut.

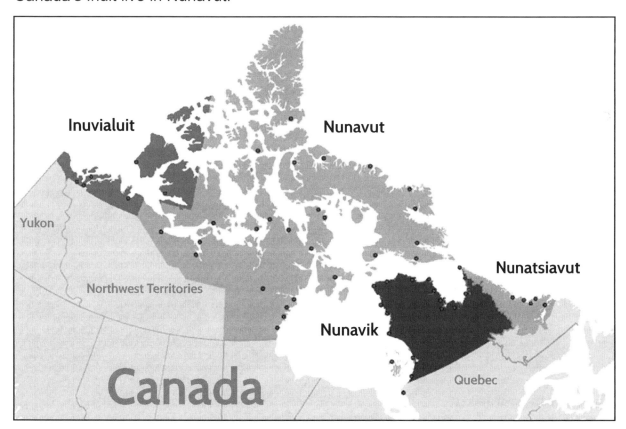

This map shows the four Inuit Regions in Canada: The Inuvialuit Region in the Northwest Territories, the territory of Nunavut, Nunavik in northern Quebec, and Nunatsiavut in northern Labrador.

The Arctic regions where the Inuit live have no trees, though there are mosses and grasses and some low bushes that have berries. The berries could be eaten or used to make teas. In summer, even though much of the Arctic is cloud-covered or foggy, daylight can last almost 24 hours—a full day! But winters in the Arctic are long and cold. Sometimes the sun appears for only a few hours. In some communities that are very far north, the sun doesn't appear at all for many weeks in mid-winter!

Way of Life

The Inuit were a semi-nomadic people, which means they moved three or four times a year. They moved with the seasons, usually to hunt. Each year, they would return to hunting and fishing spots they knew and liked. Usually, the Inuit hunted and travelled in the spring, summer, and fall.

Climate change has changed the Inuit way of life in recent years. As melting ice makes life more and more difficult for the animals of the Arctic, hunting and the traditional Inuit way of life become harder. Today, most Inuit live similar lives to those of people in the rest of Canada. However, the Inuit express their culture through various forms of art, including carving, print making, and throat singing. The Arctic Winter Games, held every two years, feature traditional Inuit sports.

Soapstone carving of an Inuit hunter

Vigilant Owl by Kenojuak Ashevak—one of Canada's best-known artists

Food

Because there are not many edible plants in the Arctic, the Inuit ate mostly meat and fish they got from hunting, fishing, or trapping. They caught caribou, musk oxen, Arctic hare, polar bear, seal, whale, walrus, duck, fox, and wolf. They fished for Arctic char, salmon, trout, and whitefish. They also gathered birds' eggs and berries. Often, food was eaten raw, but sometimes it was cooked. It could also be dried and stored in a cool area or preserved in oil. Today, the Inuit can buy some of their food in stores. But in many northern communities, fresh food such as milk, fruit, and vegetables must be brought in, usually by plane, from a long way away. Fresh food is expensive in the Arctic—in Nunavut, a single kilo of grapes can cost $28!

Caribou

Musk Oxen

Walrus

An Inuit hunter waits at a breathing hole for the seal to appear.

Clothing

Traditionally, the Inuit made their own clothing from animal skins and furs. Seal and caribou were the most common, though polar bear, fox, wolf, and even birds were also used. Men, women, and children wore hooded coats called parkas, which were often made of caribou skins. They also wore gloves or mittens and watertight boots called mukluks. The word "mukluk" comes from an Indigenous word, "maklak," which means "bearded seal." Some Inuit sewed their clothing using thread made of seal or walrus intestines, since these are waterproof.

Men, women, and children wore parkas, hooded coats often made of caribou skins.

Because it is very cold in some regions where the Inuit live, in winter they dressed in layers. Usually, clothing had an inner layer with the fur facing the skin and an outer layer with the fur facing out. On their feet the Inuit might wear three layers: a "stocking," a fur slipper, and a mukluk.

Housing

Today, most Inuit live in wooden houses clustered in small villages. But in the past, they had a summer home and a winter home. In summer the Inuit lived in tents made from animal skins, such as caribou. In winter, they lived in sod houses or igloos. A sod house had a frame made of driftwood or whalebone. Sod would be draped over this to make a roof and packed around it to make walls. Depending on where they lived, some Inuit could use driftwood logs to make their winter houses.

Beliefs

The Inuit believed that all things had spirits. Humans, animals, forces of nature (such as wind and storms), and non-living objects, such as rocks, all had spirits. Inuit myths and legends explained many things about life, for instance, how the sun, moon, and stars came into being. They also explained the existence of good and evil. To tell these myths and legends, the Inuit used stories, songs, dances, masks, and small carvings. They wanted to pass these legends on so they would be remembered and remain part of their culture.

Inuit shaman mask

Shamans

It was thought that only certain people could control the spirits. These people were called shamans. A shaman ("angakkuq") could be male or female. The Inuit believed shamans had magical powers, such as the ability to fly or turn themselves into animals. It was also thought that good shamans could cure illness by forcing evil spirits out of the body. Shamans used dances, drums, and charms to talk to the spirit world. They wore special masks while performing these rituals. The masks were carved from driftwood or bone, and usually showed an animal. The Inuit believed these masks had powers that helped the shaman talk to the spirits.

Inuit Legends

One of the most important Inuit spirits was Sedna, the goddess of the sea. The Inuit believed that Sedna controlled many of the animals who lived in the sea, such as seals, walruses, and whales. These animals were very important to the Inuit. They needed their meat, skin, tusks, and even their intestines to survive. The Inuit believed they must keep Sedna happy so she would let them continue to hunt these animals.

Stone carving of Sedna throwing a beluga whale

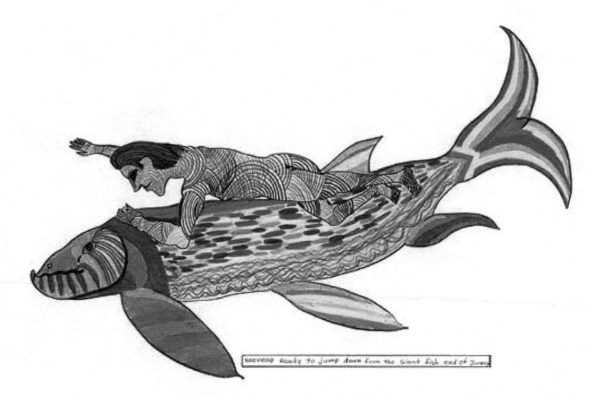

Kiviuk's Journey, illustrated by William Noah

Another Inuit spirit was Kiviuq. In Inuit mythology, Kiviuq was an eternal wanderer who roamed the Arctic and had many adventures. Kiviuq had supernatural powers. These helped him to overcome sea monsters, giants, and other challenges he met in his travels. Did you know that the planet Saturn has a moon called Kiviuq? It was named in 2003 after this important Inuit spirit.

"Peoples of the Arctic"–Think About It

1. Which four regions make up the Inuit Nunangat?

2. How often did the Inuit move in a year? Why did they move?

3. Name four kinds of animal and two kinds of fish the Inuit caught for food.

4. What are *mukluks*? Tell about the origin of the word.

5. Give two examples of the kinds of things Inuit myths and legends explained.

6. What two things did the Inuit believe about Sedna, goddess of the sea?

Peoples of the Subarctic

The Subarctic peoples lived on the largest territory of any group of First Nations peoples. The area where they lived stretched over most of northern Canada, from Yukon to Newfoundland. This group included the Gwich'in (Kutchin), Innu, Montagnais, Naskapi, Yellowknife nations and more. Life was hard for these peoples because of the long, harsh winters. Most of these First Nations moved around following the migrating animals.

Home on the Move

The peoples across this wide area created many different kinds of buildings for their homes. But all had similarities: they were small, and they were quick to set up and take down, so they could be moved easily.

Some Subarctic peoples lived in tipis. In the north where few trees grow and wood is scarce, the supports that formed the cone shape might be whale bones. Other groups lived in wigwams, which were domes formed from curved poles and covered with bark, brush, or hides.

Peoples of the Subarctic also lived in lean-tos. These are triangle-shaped buildings topped by a sharply angled roof. A pole or whale bone was lashed between two trees and shorter poles were leaned against it to make a frame. Animal hides or brush covered the frame to keep the lean-to warm.

A lean-to was made of wood and bone, and covered with brush or animal hide.

Other Subarctic peoples lived in homes called ridgepole lodges. These buildings had upright poles in the centre of the front and back, with longer poles stretched between them. Poles were leaned against these long poles from both sides, then covered with bark or skins.

Getting Around

The Subarctic peoples' survival depended on their being able to walk long distances in search of food. To transport heavy loads, they used a tumpline to lighten the heavy pack. A tumpline was a piece of cloth or animal hide that a hunter fastened around a load, then around his forehead to support the weight of the pack. Later, dogs were used to pull loads.

In summer, these peoples canoed the rivers and lakes. In winter, they wore snowshoes and used toboggans to move heavy loads.

Moose and Pike

Bear, caribou, and moose were some of the animals the men of the Subarctic hunted. They used bows and arrows, as well as traps and corrals.

Women set snares, preserved meat, and cleaned hides. It was also the women who fished, using hooks, nets, or spears to catch lake trout, pike, whitefish, and more. As well, the women picked berries, dandelions, moss, and other plants.

Animal Spirits

Many of the nations in the Subarctic believed in spirit beings and animal spirits. They told stories about Raven, who could be both a hero and a trickster. Children were taught how important it is to have good relations with the spirits of animals and with nature, since it was believed these could affect people's well-being.

Raven

In late summer, some groups held ceremonies to celebrate the harvest. Many of the nations sang songs, often accompanied by the beat of a hand drum (a drum played with the bare hand, rather than a drumstick).

"Peoples of the Subarctic"–Think About It

1. In which area of Canada did the Peoples of the Subarctic live?

2. What are the names of three of the First Nations who lived here?

3. Name four types of dwellings the Peoples of the Subarctic lived in.

4. What is a *tumpline*?

5. Which tasks did the women perform? Name three.

6. What were children taught, and why?

Farmers of the Eastern Woodlands

On the shores of Ontario's Great Lakes and the St. Lawrence River in southwestern and south central Ontario lived the Farmers of the Eastern Woodlands. These peoples included the Haudenosaunee (Iroquois), Neutral, Tionontati (Petun), Wendat (Huron), and others. The word "Ontario" comes from the Iroquois word "Onitariio," which means "Beautiful Lake."

Palisades and Longhouses

Because the land these Eastern Woodlands peoples farmed was so fertile, they didn't move around, as many other First Nations did. Instead, they stayed where they were and became farmers.

These peoples lived in villages with as many as 1,500 people in them. Each village was surrounded by walls known as palisades. These were rows of posts with sharp points, and there could be as many as three rows around a single village. Some of these settlements had platforms or watchtowers on the palisades so that sentries could keep watch for attacks from enemies.

These Eastern Woodlands people lived in longhouses, with between 20 and 200 in a village. Each home was a long, rectangular building with a rounded roof—it looked a little like an upside-down basket. Wooden poles formed the frame of the longhouse, which was then covered with tree bark.

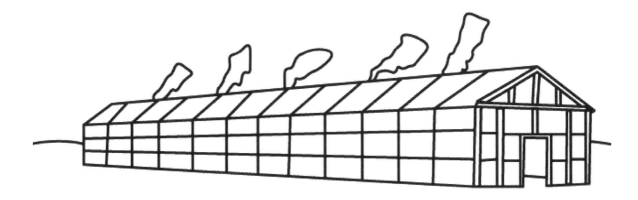

Clans and families lived in longhouses.

The Three Sisters and Other Foods

Farmers of the Eastern Woodlands were known for preparing their fields for planting by burning down the trees and brush on the land and letting the ash fertilize the soil.

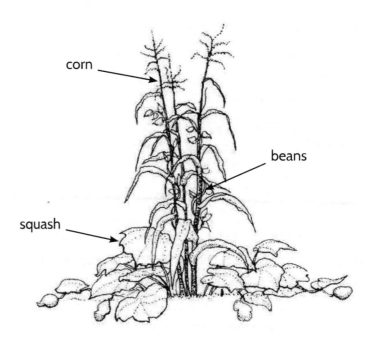

The Three Sisters

These farmers mainly planted crops known as the Three Sisters: corn, beans, and squash. The Iroquois told stories about these crops. The Corn was righteous and stood tall and straight. The shy Bean clutched the Corn's legs, while the Squash, spreading about on the ground, was the troublemaker.

Despite their differences, the Three Sisters worked together. The corn provided a support for the beans, the beans added nitrogen to the soil to enrich it, and the squash leaves shaded the ground to keep moisture in and weeds out.

Corn was a very important crop because it could be dried and made into soup to feed a village throughout the winter. Some groups even had an early type of popcorn! The husks from the corn were woven and braided to make dolls, masks, mats, and slippers.

The Eastern Woodlands peoples also gathered bark, berries, herbs, and sunflowers to eat. In the spring, they collected the sap of maple trees and boiled it to make maple syrup or maple sugar. They also hunted deer, rabbits, and water birds, and they fished the rivers and lakes.

Staying Warm

The Eastern Woodlands farmers wore clothes made from fur and animal hides, as well as from corn husks. For sewing, they used needles made from deer bones, and thread made of animal tendons or fibres from elm bark.

Men wore skirts, or kilts, made of leather in the summer and leggings in winter. Women wore deerskin dresses often belted at the waist. They also wore leggings in the winter, as well as a warm skirt.

"Farmers of the Eastern Woodlands"–Think About It

1. Where did the farmers of the Eastern Woodlands live?
2. Give another name for each of these First Nations: Iroquois, Petun, and Huron.
3. What are *palisades*?
4. Name and briefly describe the type of dwelling Eastern Woodlands farmers lived in.
5. What is the story the Iroquois told about "the Three Sisters"?
6. Which crop was important for Eastern Woodlands farmers, and why?

Hunters of the Eastern Woodlands

In southeastern Canada lived the hunters of the Eastern Woodlands. From south and southwestern Ontario, through southern Quebec, New Brunswick, Nova Scotia and Prince Edward Island to Newfoundland, these First Nations farmed some crops but mostly survived by fishing, gathering wild plants, and hunting. These peoples were known as Algonquians and included the Maliseet (Malécite), Mi'kmaq, Odawa (Ottawa), and Ojibwe (Ojibway), among other nations.

Eastern Woodland Villages

In summer, Eastern Woodlands hunters lived in small villages that could hold as few as one or two small dwellings or as many as several hundred people. Some First Nations who lived by lakes or swamps worked together to harvest wild rice. In the fall and winter, they spread out into small groups to follow and hunt wild animals.

Wigwam

Most hunters of the Eastern Woodlands lived in wigwams. These were dome-shaped homes that fit just one family and could be built and transported easily.

Birch Trees

Birch trees were very important to the hunters of the Eastern Woodlands. They used the bark to create canoes, wigwams, and baskets, among other things. Birchbark is lightweight and waterproof, and sticky oils in it make it strong and flexible. The bark could also be used to wrap and store food, or it could be rolled into a cone to make a moose call or placed on a wound to help it stop bleeding and heal faster.

Birchbark biting was a craft these First Nations practised to make intricate spiritual and religious designs. Sometimes they just partially bit through the bark and sometimes they pierced it completely to decorate boxes, drums, and other items.

Birch wood burns well, so it was often used for cooking fires. The frames for snowshoes were usually made from this strong wood. As well, these First Nations drank the sap from birch trees to help cure colds.

Birchbark strips

Gathering Meat and Medicine

Using spears or bows and arrows, the hunters of the Eastern Woodland hunted beaver, deer, moose, porcupines, and more. In winter, they used snowshoes to follow animal tracks, then hauled the meat back to their camps on toboggans.

The Eastern Woodlands peoples gathered berries, nuts, and plants not only to eat, but also for medicine. A tea made from cedar bark and leaves provided vitamin C, while the bark of the willow tree has a pain-killing drug in it.

Eastern Woodland Clothing

Most of these First Nations wore clothes made of animal, bird, or fish skins. Deerskin was especially popular because there were many deer in the area. These hunters wore pelts, which are animal skins that still have fur on them, or hides, which are skins with no fur. The skins could be processed to make leather that was sewn into dresses, leggings, moccasins, shirts, and robes. In cold weather the Eastern Woodlands peoples wore mittens, heavy coats, and warm hats.

Women made the clothes for their families and often decorated it with feathers, paint, shells, stones, and embroidery made using porcupine quills.

"Hunters of the Eastern Woodlands"–Think About It

1. Aside from farming, how did the hunters of the Eastern Woodlands survive?
2. What name were these peoples known by?
3. Which crop did First Nations who lived by lakes or swamps harvest?
4. What did the Eastern Woodlands hunters use birchbark for? Name six things.
5. What were cedar tree bark and willow tree bark used for?
6. What is the difference between pelts and hides?

Names of Indigenous Peoples

There are many Indigenous groups across the country. Many of their names mean "the people" in their languages, including Beothuk (pronounced *Bee-oh-thuk*), Haida (pronounced *High-dah*), Innu (pronounced *In-noo*), Inuit (pronounced *In-noo-it*), and Salish (pronounced *Say-lish*). Here are some of the other well-known Indigenous groups in Canada and what their names mean.

Peoples of the West Coast and Plains

The Indigenous peoples known by English speakers as Tlingit (pronounced *Kling-kit*) call themselves Lingit (pronounced *Ling-kit*), which means "people of the tides." This group depended on the ocean and its plants and animals for survival. The Lingit word *Naas*, which means "food depot," was given to the Nass River in northern British Columbia. The name refers to the great number of fish they could catch there in the spring, which fed a great many people. The Indigenous name *Nisga'a* (pronounced *Niss-gaah*) means "people of the Nass River."

Lillooet (pronounced *Li-low-wet*) means "wild onion" and is a name given to an Indigenous group that lived where this plant grew well. The name *Shuswap* (pronounced *Shoo-swop*) was created by fur traders who could not pronounce the group's name, Secwepemc (pronounced *sheh-whep-m*), which means "downriver."

Peoples of the Plains

The Siksika (pronounced *Sik-sikah*) are also known as the Blackfoot. *Siksika* means "black foot." The name refers to the dark moccasins that these Indigenous peoples wore.

Chipewyan (pronounced *Chip-ah-why-an*) is a name that means "pointed skins." It comes from the way these peoples dried beaver skins, which created points on the parkas made from them. The Chipewyans call themselves *Dene* (pronounced *Deh-nay*), which means "people."

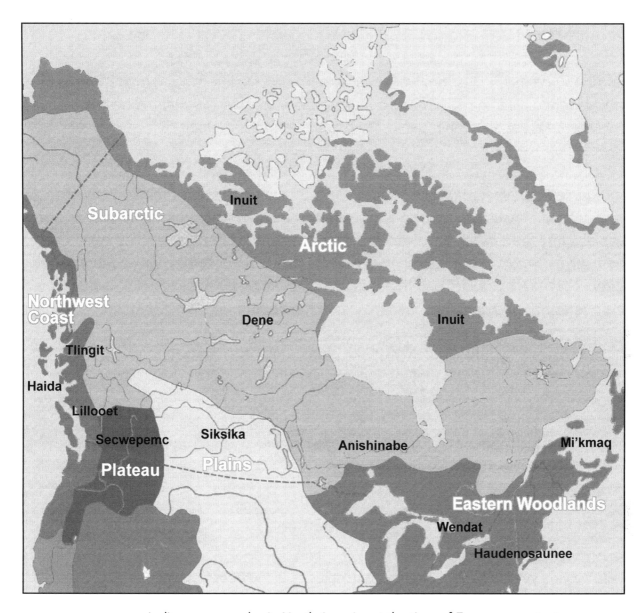

Indigenous peoples in North America at the time of European contact

People of the Woodlands

Huron (pronounced *Hyer-on*) was the name French explorers gave to the Wendat, or Wyandot (pronounced *Why-an-dot*) Indigenous peoples. *Huron* means "wild boar" in French. *Wyandot* means "peninsula people," and they originally lived in the St. Lawrence Valley.

The name *Iroquois* (pronounced *Ear-oh-kwah)*) comes from a word meaning "real snakes." It was an insulting name given to the people by their enemies, and was used by the English and French settlers. These Indigenous peoples called themselves *Haudenosaunee* (pronounced *Ho-dee-no-show-nee*), which means "people of the longhouse" and refers to the style of homes they lived in. Today, they are one of six Indigenous groups that joined together to form the Six Nations.

In the Maritimes and Eastern Woodlands, the name *Mi'kmaq* (pronounced *mee-gmakh*) came from a word that means "my friends." The Ojibway or Ojibwe (both pronounced *Oh-jib-way*) people got their name from a word meaning "puckered." It refers to the puckered moccasins they wore. The Ojibway call themselves *Anishinabe* (pronounced *A-nish-shin-aw-bay*), which means "original people."

"Names of Indigenous Peoples"–Think About It

1. How did the Ojibway get their name?
2. Why do you think some Indigenous peoples have more than one name?
3. If someone insults you by calling you a snake, what characteristics do they think you have?
4. The Chipewyans got their name from the way they dressed. What are some other features that gave Indigenous peoples their names?
5. Why was the Nass River so important to the Nisga'a people?
6. What are three interesting facts you learned from this text?

Who Are the Wendat?

The Wendat (or Ouendat) lived in what is now southern Ontario, where the towns of Barrie, Orillia, and Penetanguishene are. Because of where their territory was located, the Wendat are part of a larger group of Indigenous people known as Peoples of the Eastern Woodland. The name Wendat means "people who live on the back of a great turtle."

Life in a Longhouse

A Wendat village was usually located on a hill that had a marsh or swamp around the bottom. These features made the village easy to defend and the Wendat could easily see enemies approaching. As well, each village was surrounded by as many as three palisades—rows of closely spaced posts with sharp, pointed ends.

Wendat village surrounded by palisades

Inside the village, the Wendat lived in longhouses. There could be as many as 100 longhouses in a Wendat village. These were large, rectangular homes with rounded roofs. Poles and logs formed the frame of these homes, which were then covered with cedar, fir, or spruce bark. Some of these homes could fit more than ten families.

Inside a longhouse were compartments for each family. There were raised sleeping platforms along the walls, with bearskins for blankets. Cooking fires were located in a row down the centre of the longhouse.

Hunting, Gathering, Planting

The Wendat fished and hunted, as well as picking fruit and gathering herbs, nuts, and roots. This group of Indigenous people is one of the few who also grew food. To clear a field and make it ready to plant a crop, the Wendat burned the trees and grass where they wanted to plant. The ash from the fire fertilized the soil.

The main crops that the Wendat planted were beans, corn, and squash (the Three Sisters). The beans grew tall, supported by the corn stalks, while the wide leaves of the squash shaded the ground and made it hard for weeds to grow.

The Wendat made sure their villages were close to a good water supply to help their crops grow. But every 10 to 15 years, the crops would use up the nutrients in the soil and all the nearby firewood would have been cut down. The villagers had to move and rebuild their palisades and longhouses in a new location.

The Wendat Today

Explorers from France met the Wendat beginning in the 1500s. The Frenchmen called these Indigenous people the "Huron." The name comes from the French word "hure" and means "wild boar." The French gave the Wendat this nickname because the Indigenous men's bristly hairstyle reminded the French of the wild animal.

Unfortunately, contact with the Europeans exposed the Wendat to diseases, and many of them died. After 1650, the peoples of the Wendat confederacy were scattered from their lands as a result of battles with the Haudenosaunee (Iroquois). The surviving Wendat joined other nations but kept their own identity. Today, descendants of these people mostly live mostly on the Wendake Reserve, which is near Quebec City in the province of Quebec.

"Who Are the Wendat"–Think About It

1. What does the name *Wendat* mean?
2. Where were Wendat villages usually located, and why?
3. How many families could fit in a large longhouse?
4. How did the Wendat make a field ready for planting?
5. Why did the Wendat have to pack up and move every 10 or 15 years?
6. Why did the French give the Wendat the nickname *Huron*?

The League of Six Nations

Between 600 and 700 years ago, five of the Eastern Woodlands farming nations formed a military and political association known as a confederacy. These five nations were the Cayuga, Kanienkehaka (Mohawk), Oneida, Onondaga, and Seneca. In the 1700s, the Tuscarora nation joined, so the confederacy became known as the League of Six Nations.

Clans, Matrons, and Sachems

There were nine clans in the League of Six Nations: Bear, Beaver, Deer, Eel, Hawk, Heron, Snipe, Turtle, and Wolf. Each family in the clan had a clan mother, or matron, and each of these women chose a chief, or sachem, to speak for her family. Since the women put the sachems into power, they could remove them if they didn't do a good job.

There were 50 sachems on the Grand Council who created the laws for the league. Important issues were discussed by all of the sachems, and decisions were made only when a majority agreed.

In Onondaga, in what is now New York State, was the council house where the Grand Council met and the confederacy's records were kept.

Symbols of the Six Nations

A pine tree is still the symbol of the League of Six Nations. The roots of the tree are an important part of the symbol, and they are shown spreading out in all directions. This represents how any person looking for peace can follow the roots and find the shelter of the great peace. High atop the tree, an eagle stands guard. It protects anyone who takes shelter under the pine tree.

Carefully woven sashes known as wampum belts documented agreements, ceremonies, and treaties. Made of hand-drilled and polished shells, wampum belts worked as memory guides to help the elders recite the history of the Six Nations. The condolence cane is a symbol of great authority within the Six Nations and is still used today. Listed on the cane are the fifty sachems in the confederacy.

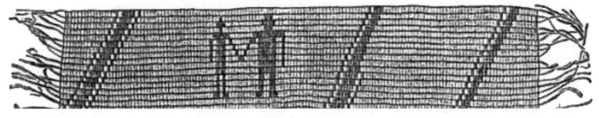

wampum belt

The Great Law of Peace

At ceremonial events, a story was often told of how the League of Six Nations was formed. Long ago, there was a time of constant war for the farmers of the Eastern Woodlands. Many people lost their lives and it seemed that the war would never end. Finally, two people named Deganawideh (also called The Great Peacemaker) and Hiawatha started to talk about bringing peace to the peoples.

The two men talked and negotiated for many years. Finally, they were able to bring the five nations together to form a league. It was based on the Great Law of Peace, or the Gayanashagowa.

Under the Great Law of Peace, people are viewed as being members of one family. This family has just one body, one heart, and one mind. Freedom, harmony, and peace are all important parts of the Great Law of Peace.

Today, about 50,000 Six Nations people live in Canada. The Six Nations reserve is the largest First Nations reserve in Canada. It is located near Brantford, in southwestern Ontario.

"The League of Six Nations"–Think About It

1. Which nations formed the League of Six Nations?
2. What is a *sachem*? What was the sachem's role?
3. What do the spreading roots of the pine tree represent?
4. What did Deganawideh and Hiawatha achieve?
5. How does the Great Law of Peace see people and the family?
6. Where is Canada's largest First Nations reserve located?

The Métis

Canada's Métis are people who descended from both First Nations and European people. The name Métis was first used in the mid-1600s, when First Nations began marrying Europeans. The groups met because the Indigenous people helped the Europeans with the fur trade. The Métis live mostly in Alberta, Saskatchewan, Manitoba, and Ontario. Today there are about 600,000 Métis in Canada.

Capots and Ceintures Fléchées

Fur traders depended on the Métis to guide them through the Canadian wilderness, help them live in the woods, and supply them with pemmican. This was food made from dried meat, melted fat, and berries, which lasted well on the trails. The Métis could speak the languages of many groups and were excellent buffalo hunters.

The Métis wore a combination of Indigenous and European styles. The men were dressed in moccasins, deerskin pants, and a long coat called a capot (pronounced *ka-poe*). Around his waist, a Métis man would often wear a specially woven sash known as a *ceinture fléchée* (*san-toor flesh-ay*) — it means "arrowed sash." Because the sashes could be used to carry items like rope and saddle blankets, among other things, they became very important and today are a symbol of the Métis.

Métis originals

Fiddle-playing and step-dancing are two things that the Métis are known for. The music and dancing began with the French and Scots, but the Métis added their unique flavour. They made their own fiddles and included steps from First Nations dances.

Métis beadwork is also famous. Using tiny beads, the Métis created beautiful flowers on bags, gloves, jackets, and more. As well, Métis crafters embroidered flowers from silk thread.

The Red River cart was also invented by the Métis. This was a large, two-wheeled cart that had no metal in it at all—nails were very expensive in those days. This cart was light enough to float across streams but could still carry heavy loads.

Louis Riel

The most famous Métis is Louis Riel. He was a leader in the Métis Red River Settlement in what is today Manitoba. In 1868 he feared the Hudson's Bay Company was about to give Canada a huge chunk of that land. The Métis weren't consulted, so Riel and his followers moved in to stop Canadian officials from entering the settlement.

Riel tried to negotiate with the Canadian government but when talks failed, the Métis fought against settlers and soldiers for the land. This was known as the Red River Rebellion or the Red River Resistance.

Louis Riel, circa 1873

In 1869, Canada recognized Métis rights and created the province of Manitoba, with Riel as its leader. But during the Rebellion, Riel's government had hanged a non-Métis man. After leading a second Métis rebellion (the Northwest Rebellion) in 1885, Riel turned himself in to the Canadian militia and eventually was hanged for treason. Was Riel a hero for defending western Canada? It is still debated by some Canadians.

"The Metis"–Think About It

1. In which four provinces do the Métis mostly live?
2. For which three things did the fur traders depend on the Métis?
3. What is a *ceinture fléchée*, and why was it important to the Métis?
4. What did Louis Riel do in 1868, and why?
5. What did the Canadian government do in 1869?
6. Do you think Louis Riel was a hero? Explain your thinking.

Indigenous Peoples of Canada © Chalkboard Publishing Inc.

Indigenous Culture

There are many ways to learn about Indigenous peoples in Canada—their history, traditions, and culture.

Artifacts and Pictures

Archeologists and others who study ancient civilizations have found many artifacts and items that belonged to long-ago Indigenous peoples. Through archeological digs to uncover Indigenous villages and dwellings, scientists have learned about how Indigenous peoples built their homes, what materials they used, and more.

By examining items such as tools and weapons found in the buried dwellings, experts can learn a lot about how these peoples lived. The patterns of wear on the items give clues about how they were used. Clothing made from animal skins might reveal what kinds of animals lived in various areas at different times in Canada's history.

Indigenous peoples created wampum belts made of shell beads to record treaties and other historic events. The shell beads were also used as money. These artifacts tell scientists about the relationships that groups of Indigenous peoples had with each other and with Europeans.

Paintings and photographs can tell a lot about Indigenous peoples who lived long ago. For instance, the way they are dressed may indicate a special occasion. The decorations on clothes or moccasins can tell what was important.

Pictographs and Petroglyphs

Sometimes Indigenous peoples painted pictures on rock walls. These images are called *pictographs*. Usually the pictures were drawn with a red paint made from crushed rock. Sometimes the artists used black, white, or yellow paints made from other ingredients. Using brushes or their fingers, the Indigenous peoples drew human figures, animals, abstract designs, hunting scenes, and more.

Indigenous peoples also carved patterns and pictographs into cliff walls and boulders using stone tools. These are called *petroglyphs*.

Pictographs

 Indigenous Peoples of Canada © Chalkboard Publishing Inc.

Legends and Stories

Indigenous peoples have a strong tradition of passing along wisdom and knowledge in story form. The information and stories are passed down from generation to generation so they are not forgotten.

Elders tell legends to children and other members of their community. This keeps their history and culture alive and helps draw Indigenous peoples together. The stories tell of the beginnings of the First Nation, how they survived difficult times, or how big events changed their lives. These tales give the young people ideas about coping with similar situations now and in the future.

"Indigenous Culture"–Think About It!

1. Using information from this text and your own ideas, what are some ways to learn about Indigneous culture?
2. What is the difference between *pictographs* and *petroglyphs*?
3. Why is it important to pass along Indigenous legends? Explain your thinking.
4. What can archeological digs tell scientists about Indigenous groups?
5. What are *wampum belts*?
6. Use the pictographs to write a message.

Indigenous Communities

Indigenous communities were organized along family lines. They were based on the links between people who were brothers and sisters, parents and children, or uncles and aunts, as well as on the ties created by marriage.

Elders

Perhaps the most important people in any Indigenous community were the elders. These men and women were the teachers, the people who held the knowledge and passed it along. Elders advised leaders so choices could be made that were best for the whole community.

Decisions were made by consensus (general agreement). Many Indigenous communities still use talking circles to make decisions. In a talking circle, everyone is equal and there is no leader.

From the elders, the other adults and the children in the community learned about their history, culture, and traditions. The children were also taught by the elders about their responsibilities to the community, in particular, having respect for all of creation and the gifts the Creator had given them.

A symbol for a talking circle. The person holding the "talking feather" is the only person allowed to speak. The feather is then passed to another person.

Adults

Indigenous men and women shared the responsibility of feeding the community. The men fished and hunted, especially larger animals such as moose and bears. The men traded with other Indigenous groups and built homes. When it was necessary, men also fought other Indigenous groups to protect their community or to expand it.

Men in Indigenous communities also cleared land and made it ready for planting. Indigenous women planted and harvested the crops. The women prepared the animals for eating, and dried and scraped the animal skins so they could be used to make clothing.

Women hunted small animals and birds, and also gathered berries, nuts, and other foods from the forests around them.

Children

Indigenous children were cared for by the entire community. From an early age, children were taught skills that they would need as adults. For example, boys played games that taught them what they would need to know to fish and hunt successfully. Fathers, brothers, uncles, and grandfathers passed on their knowledge in this way.

Girls needed to learn how to cook food, prepare animal skins, and sew clothing. They were taught these important skills by their mothers, sisters, aunts, and grandmothers.

"Indigenous Communities"–Think About It

1. Describe the organization of Indigenous communities. Do you think this is a good way to organize communities? Give three reasons why or why not.
2. List at least three things that Indigenous elders do.
3. What skills did Indigenous girls learn?
4. What skills did Indigenous boys learn?
5. What is a *talking circle* and how does it work?

(continued next page)

"Indigenous Communities"–Think About It

6. Complete the table to compare the responsibilities of Indigenous men and Indigenous women.

Responsibilities of Indigenous Men	Both	Responsibilities of Indigenous Women

Tipis, Longhouses, and Igloos

Across Canada, Indigenous people built many kinds of houses. They used the trees, animal skins, and other building materials around them to create homes that worked well in their environments.

Home on the Move

The most famous Indigenous house is the tipi. These were built by many First Nations, but especially those who lived on the Prairies, such as the Nehiyawak (also known as Plains Cree), Pikuni (Peigan), and Siksika (Blackfoot). Tipis were built using a number of poles made from pine trees. They were tied together at the top, then stood up to form a cone. A buffalo hide was draped over the frame and fastened in place at the top.

Tipis were easy to transport and could be set up quickly. The people of the Plains built tipis because these people travelled a lot, following the herds of buffalo.

A Siksika (Blackfoot) tipi. The dark portion at the top represents the sky, the dark band at the bottom represents the earth.

Pit Houses

The First Nations who lived in southeastern British Columbia built lodges, tents, and tipis, like many other First Nations. But during the winter, the Ktunaxa (Kootenay), Secwepemc (Shuswap), Stl'atl'imx (Lillooet) and other peoples of the area created pit houses that were partly underground.

Pit houses were dome shaped, with only the top part of the dwelling visible. The roof was framed with poles, then covered with tree boughs and earth. This home had a side door, as well as a hole in the roof. A ladder made from a notched log led down from the roof hole to the floor of the home. Several families might live in each pit house, sharing a cooking fire in the middle.

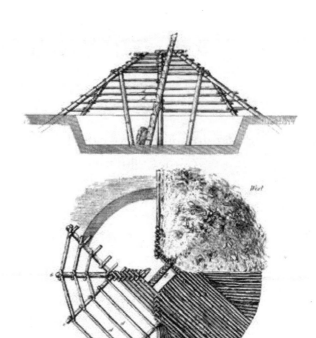

Pit houses were the winter underground dwellings of the Plateau peoples. The only entrance was at the top. A ladder was used to enter the pit house.

Homes Built of Snow

Another well-known Indigenous dwelling is the igloo. In the Arctic there are no trees, so the Inuit had to use another building material: snow. Carefully selecting snow—it had to be soft enough to chop into blocks but packed enough to be easily moved—Inuit cut snow blocks with specially designed knives made from ivory, bone, or metal.

Igloo made from hard snow blocks

Skilled snow cutters chopped each block so it would fit perfectly into the igloo's dome shape. Soft snow was packed into the cracks between the blocks and a vent hole at the top of the dome let heat and smoke out.

Some Inuit used igloos only when travelling. Others lived in them through the whole winter. Sometimes an igloo took only 40 minutes to build! But if they were going to live in it all winter, the Inuit built a bigger igloo. This could take up to two days.

Watch a real igloo being built at this website:
http://www.nfb.ca/film/how_to_build_an_igloo/

Life in a Longhouse

First Nations who lived in central Canada (today's Ontario) and on the west coast all built large houses called longhouses. On the coast, the houses built by the Gitxsan, Haida, and Nisga'a could be big enough to accommodate up to 60 people. These boxy structures were made from cedar trees and usually had one doorway, which faced the shore.

Iroquoian peoples, including the Cayuga, Onondaga, and Wendat, also built longhouses, but these were usually just for five or six families. Like the west coast longhouses, they were rectangular; however, these featured rounded roofs that were covered with elm, ash, or fir bark.

"Tipis, Longhouses, and Igloos"–Think About It

1. Name three First Nations who built tipis.
2. Why were tipis a good type of dwelling for the peoples of the Plains?
3. What type of home did the Ktunaxa, the Secwepemc, and the Stl'atl'imx live in in winter?
4. Why did the Inuit have to use snow to build their dwellings?
5. Why do you think the longhouses of the west coast had a doorway that faced the shore? Explain your ideas.
6. How did the longhouses built in central Canada differ from those out west?

Getting Around—Transportation

Indigenous people have had many ways to travel across their territories. How they got around depended on the materials they found around them for building boats and other vehicles.

On Water

Many Indigenous people used canoes to paddle along rivers and lakes. On the west coast, Indigenous people created dugout canoes from huge cedar trees. They carved the tree using special tools to make a sturdy canoe that could stand up to the ocean's huge waves.

The Peoples of the Plateau, who lived in southeastern British Columbia, made dugout canoes too. The Ktunaxa people of the area built sturgeon-nosed canoes. A sturgeon is a long-nosed fish. These canoes got their name because they had long bows (fronts) and sterns (backs).

The Indigenous peoples who live in what is now Ontario, Quebec, and the Maritimes made their canoes using birchbark. They built a wooden frame for the canoe, then wrapped it in the bark. Birchbark is thin and easy to mould, as well as tough and water-resistant.

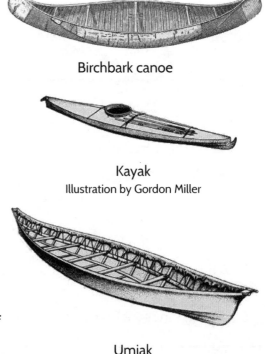

Birchbark canoe

Kayak
Illustration by Gordon Miller

Umiak
Illustration by Gordon Miller

In the Arctic, the Inuit used skin-covered boats called umiaks and kayaks. "Umiak" means "open-skinned boat." Umiaks were large boats, usually made of animal skin, such as walrus, stretched over a driftwood or whalebone frame. Up to 20 people could fit in an umiak, which could be 10 metres long. Kayaks were smaller, lighter, and faster. Kayaks were usually made of seal or caribou hide stretched over a driftwood frame. A kayak was so light that a man could

Indigenous Peoples of Canada © Chalkboard Publishing Inc.

carry it over his head. This meant he could walk over ice to open water to hunt or fish. Like the umiak, the kayak today is rarely used for hunting, but it is an important part of Inuit culture. Many non-Indigenous people still use kayaks just for fun to explore Canada's lakes and rivers.

Over Land

Indigenous people walked long distances. They didn't have horses to ride or carry their belongings until the 1700s. First Nations who lived on the Prairies travelled a lot following the buffalo. To move their goods they built frames called travois. These were made by tying pine poles together to form a V-shape. Then they loaded on their belongings and harnessed the travois to a dog or, later, a horse.

Some Indigenous peoples moved heavy loads using a tumpline. This was a harness that a man or woman fastened around the forehead to distribute the weight of a large back pack.

A tumpline is a strap attached at both ends to a load placed on a person's back. By placing the strap over the top of the head, the spine, rather than the shoulders, carries the weight.

On Snow

Many groups of Indigenous people used snowshoes to get around during the winter. They came in many different shapes. Some snowshoes were long and narrow and could be longer than most people are tall! These were used by hunters as they ran over unbroken snow. Most people wore wider, more rounded snowshoes.

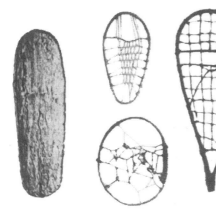  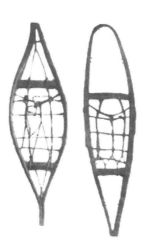

Snowshoes were made in many shapes and sizes.

Toboggans were also used by Indigenous peoples across Canada to move loads over snow. Usually the toboggans were made of wood, but some peoples in the north used the leg skins of caribou and moose. Often women pulled the toboggans, but after Europeans arrived with large breeds of dogs, heavy loads were moved by dogs.

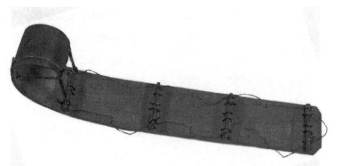

Toboggans were usually made of wood, but caribou and moose skin were also used.

Peoples of the Far North walked or used dog sleds. These sleds were not held together with nails or pins, because the bumpy, icy, frozen ground would have knocked them out of the sleds. Instead, the pieces were lashed together using animal hide. Sometimes, when no wood could be found for the sled runners, the Inuit used frozen fish lined up and wrapped in animal skin. The sleds were pulled by a team of dogs—sometimes as many as 16. They could travel long distances this way. Many Inuit now use snowmobiles to get around, so the dog sled is not used as much. But some Inuit keep teams of dogs that they use for racing.

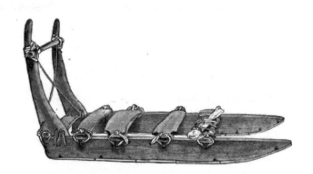

Walrus bone sled

"Getting Around–Transportation"–Think About It

1. Name two types of trees that were used to make canoes.
2. What does *umiak* mean?
3. Why was it significant that the kayak was so light?
4. Why did Indigenous people have to walk long distances before the 1700s?
5. Name three types of transportation Indigenous peoples used on snow.
6. Why were sleds in the Far North not built using nails or pins? What was used instead?

The Women of the Haudenosaunee Confederacy

Five nations made up the original Haudenosaunee (pronounced *Ho-dee-no-show-nee*) Confederacy. They were the Mohawk, Oneida, Onondaga, Cayuga, and Seneca. The confederacy was formed many, many years ago. It was formed so these nations could live in peace with each other. In 1714, the Tuscarora Nation joined the confederacy. Each nation had its own chief and council. The confederacy had a Grand Council to deal with matters that affected all the nations.

You may know about some of the confederacy's famous leaders, such as Peacemaker, Aiionwatcha (Hiawatha), and Joseph Brant. You may also know about the Great Law of Peace. This law provided a way to settle differences using thinking and negotiations rather than violence and warfare. But you may not know about the role of women in the confederacy.

Women and the Clan System

In each nation, there were clans. A clan was like a family. Every person in a clan was related to everyone else in the clan because they shared a common female ancestor. The clan someone belonged to was passed down from mother to child. So, when a woman married a man of a different clan, their children belonged to the mother's clan. But they would also be part of the father's family.

Clans in the Haudenosaunee Confederacy are matrilineal. *Matri* comes from the Latin word for "mother." *Lineal* means "a direct line."

Women also owned the land where crops were grown. They tended the crops. When a woman married, her husband moved into the house of his wife's family.

The Clan Mother was the leader of the clan. The Clan Mother was usually the oldest woman in the clan. She had the responsibility of choosing the chief of her clan and making sure he did a good job. It was also her task to make sure everyone in the clan was well-fed.

Haudenosaunee Matrilineal Clan Structure

In a matrilineal structure, descent and inheritance is passed from the mother to her female descendants.

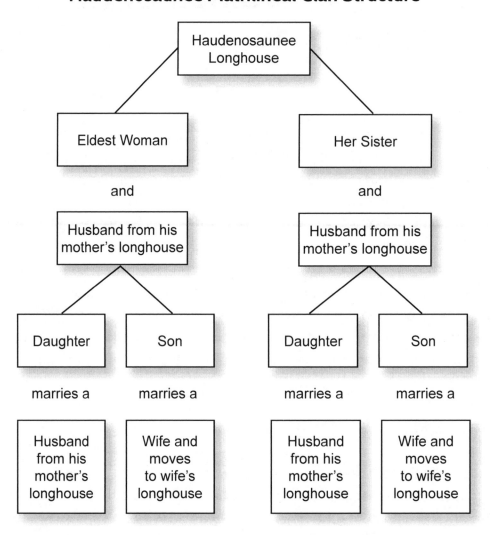

The clan system is still part of the Haudenosaunee Confederacy today. Women still have strong roles. Property is inherited through women. The Clan Mothers still select chiefs and provide advice and guidance.

"The Women of the Haudenosaunee Confederacy"–Think About It

1. A *confederacy* is an agreement between people or groups for a common purpose. How does this relate to the Haudenosaunee Confederacy?

2. What did the Grand Council do? What do you think each nation's council did?

3. Why is *matrilineal* a good word to describe the confederacy's clans?

4. Why was the Great Law of Peace important?

5. Which five nations made up the original Haudenosaunee Confederacy?

Indigenous People and the Environment

Long ago, Indigenous people depended on the land around them for everything they needed. They made food, building supplies, clothing, medicine, and more from the resources they found around them.

Gifts of the Creator

Indigenous people believe that the land where they live and its animals, plants, and other resources are gifts from the Creator. They respect these gifts and teach their children to take only what they need. Treating nature with respect is the Indigenous people's way of life. It is part of their traditions and spiritual beliefs. This respect affects how they work and play together, and is a part of who they are.

To survive, Indigenous people had to understand how all parts of the environment were connected to other parts and to their own lives. They still believe that humans are part of the environment, not separate from it. Indigenous people also feel that all living creatures are equal to humans and deserve respect.

Food from the Land

Long ago, Indigenous people were able to survive because they used the gifts of the Creator that they found around them. They tapped maple trees to make maple syrup, and gathered berries, nuts, fruit, mushrooms, wild rice, herbs, and edible roots. Indigenous people who were farmers appreciated rich soil, quenching rains, and warm sun for their crops.

Indigenous men fished, and hunted animals such as moose, deer, and buffalo. The women snared rabbits, fished, and gathered the eggs of wild birds. Medicine men healed their people using medicines and treatments made from plant leaves, bark, berries, and roots.

More Gifts

Indigenous people built their homes from wood and bark. They also made sleds and canoes from wood and bark. To form snowshoes, they used wood and leather lacing they made from animal hides and guts.

When a Indigenous hunter killed an animal, he used every part of it out of respect for that animal. Indigenous women made needles out of the bones and used them with thread made from dried animal guts to sew hides together to make clothing. They made warm coats, mittens, and leggings from furs, and sewed hides into moccasins and other clothing.

Women crushed berries, flowers, and fruits to make dyes for colourful designs. They decorated clothing with porcupine quills, shells, beads, and feathers.

"Indigenous People and the Environment"–Think About It

1. As we have seen, Indigenous people depended on the land around them for everything they needed. They made food, building supplies, clothing, medicine, and more from the resources they found around them.

    How is daily life different in Canada today? What do people do to get everything they need? Use your own ideas to explain.

2. List some of the foods that Indigenous people hunted and gathered.
3. How did Indigenous people use wood and bark?
4. How did Indigenous people show respect for animals they caught?
5. List three things that you learned from this text that you did not know before.

 Indigenous Peoples of Canada © Chalkboard Publishing Inc.

Indigenous Inventions

Indigenous people were the first to farm North America, to travel around it, and to build a civilization here. Like people everywhere, they created inventions to make their lives easier. Many of these inventions are still used today.

Getting Around

The Inuit needed a way to travel through the cold seas that surrounded them, so, about 4,000 years ago, they invented the kayak. The narrow, lightweight boat is pointed at both ends and easy to move, and the paddle that propels it through the water has a blade on each end. Inventors have to use the materials that are available to them, so Inuit builders stretched seal skins over wooden or whalebone frames to make the kayaks.

First Nations near rivers and lakes created canoes to get around. Some used birchbark to cover the wooden frame, while First Nations on the west coast created dugout canoes by hollowing out huge logs. Indigenous people also invented the travois, and the snowshoes they created made winter travel faster and easier.

M-m-m-maple Syrup

Hundreds of years ago, Indigenous people learned how to boil sap from sugar maple trees to make sweet syrup. Today, people also make syrup from birch tree sap. Indigenous people showed European settlers how to boil the syrup and pour it on snow to make maple syrup candy.

More importantly, Indigenous people taught settlers how to make a tea from cedar bark and leaves. The drink was full of vitamin C and saved the lives of many explorers and pioneers. Indigenous people also shared their secret of freezing and drying some foods to keep them from spoiling.

Those Pesky Bugs

North America's forests are full of biting insects in the spring and summer, so it is no wonder that Indigenous people invented ways to deal with them. They invented insect repellents using herbs, oils from cedar trees, a substance made from birchbark, and more. Using roots, leaves, and bark, they also created liquids and pastes to put on skin to take away the itch after the bite.

What Else?

You may think of sunglasses as being especially useful in the summer, but the Inuit originally invented them to prevent snow blindness in winter. The goggles they created were made from bone, and had a narrow slit cut on each side to see through. These goggles reduced the amount of light that could enter the wearer's eyes.

Animal bone sunglasses

First Nations created many other inventions, ranging from the game of lacrosse (it was originally called *baggattaway*) to diapers (they used soft, absorbent moss), and even the Jolly Jumper to entertain babies!

"Indigenous Inventions"–Think About It

1. What features of the kayak make it suitable for travelling through icy, cold water? How do you think these features function?

2. What are two things that Indigenous people discovered could be done with maple sap?

3. Many of the inventions listed in the text were created to help people get around. Why do you think it is important for people to be able to get around quickly and easily?

4. What is vitamin C? Where do you get get vitamin C in your diet? Why do you think it was important for the First Nations to find a way to get vitamin C in their diets?

The First Visitors to Turtle Island

For many, many years, Indigenous people lived alone on Turtle Island, or North America. Then, about 1,000 years ago, the first visitors came to Turtle Island. These explorers were the Vikings, who came from Scandinavia in Northern Europe.

Trying to Survive

The Vikings were traders and pirates—the word "Viking" comes from an old English word for pirate. They were good sailors and had sailed as far as North Africa and Central Asia. But no one from Europe had ever travelled to Turtle Island.

The Vikings landed on the northern part of Turtle Island, on what is now Newfoundland. They built a settlement on the coast, on a site known today as L'Anse aux Meadows. This name likely comes from a French word meaning "Jellyfish Cove," but the area also has many meadows.

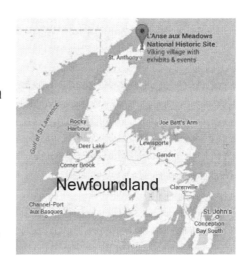

The Vikings didn't know how to survive the harsh winters in this area they called Vinland. They would have perished without the assistance of the Beothuk, the Indigenous people already living there.

The Beothuk showed the visitors where to fish and how to hunt. As well, the Vikings were taught which plants could be eaten and which ones could be used for medicine. The Beothuk taught the Scandinavians how to build homes, how to dry and prepare animals skins, and more.

The two groups also traded with each other. The Beothuk bartered food (especially fish), building materials, and clothes, including furs. From the Vikings, the Beothuk received weapons, food, and iron tools, such as axes. The Vikings also traded with the Inuit for narwhal tusks, which the Scandinavians used for carvings. A narwhal is a small Arctic whale.

The Beothuk Help Out

At L'Anse aux Meadows, the Vikings built and repaired their boats. Many tall trees grew in the area and they were carved into masts, oars, and planks. The Beothuk shared their knowledge of the best routes through the forest for moving the logs.

The Beothuk and the Vikings worked together peacefully. Treaties between the groups were made by simply shaking hands. This is how the Beothuk made treaties with other Indigenous groups.

The Vikings stayed on Turtle Island for only about ten years. Fighting broke out between the Beothuk and the Vikings, and the visitors couldn't survive in the wintry climate. But the Beothuk passed on tales of the pirates from across the water and the Vikings told legends of their time in L'Anse aux Meadows.

This is thought to be a portrait of Shawnadithit, the last known suriving Beothuk, around 1800–1829

L'Anse aux Meadows Today

Years passed and the Viking settlement was overgrown, forgotten, and lost. But in 1960 it was discovered again. Scientists found a series of mounds covered with grass and realized they were the sites of houses that the Beothuk had helped the Vikings build.

In 1978 the Viking settlement at L'Anse aux Meadows was named a World Heritage Site. Scientists agree that it is the only confirmed Norse site in North America. Today it is a symbol of the relationship between the Beothuk and Vikings on Turtle Island.

"The First Visitors to Turtle Island"–Think About It

1. Where did the first explorers to North America come from, and when?
2. What was the name of the settlement built on the east coast?
3. Name six ways in which the Beothuk helped the newcomers.
4. What did the Beothuk receive from the Vikings?
5. How did the Beothuk make treaties? Do you think this is a good way?
6. What happened in 1960?

Why Explorers Came to Canada

The Northwest Passage

For hundreds of years, Europeans had traded with India and China for silk, spices, tea, and more. The route the traders took became known as the Silk Road. But the journey over the lands through Europe and Asia was very long. Bandits and robbers also made it very dangerous. Traders began to wonder if there was a different way to reach China.

Explorers set out to discover if they could sail to China. They had no idea that an entire continent lay between them and Asia. In fact, when early explorers first came to North America, they thought they *had* reached China.

When the explorers discovered they were not in China, they began looking for a way to go over the top of Canada. They called this route the Northwest Passage. They had no idea how big Canada was or how icy the waters to the north were.

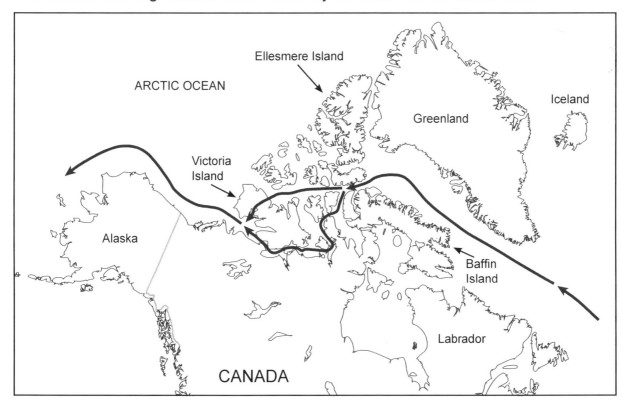

There is more than one route through the Northwest Passage. The Norwegian explorer Roald Amundsen went south of Victoria Island, and later explorers stayed to the north of the island.

Competition

Most European countries competed with each other for wealth and power. They felt it was important to own and control more land. The rulers of England and France paid for many explorers to head out and claim new lands. A lot of these explorers came to Canada. They built settlements here to help strengthen their countries' claims to the land.

European countries also wanted to spread their religion. Many missionaries came to Canada, hoping to convert Indigenous peoples to Christianity.

Fish and Fur

Early explorers were amazed at the natural resources in Canada. They fished the waters off Newfoundland, salted the fish and dried it in the sun, then shipped the fish back to Europe to help feed the people there.

Canada's huge trees provided lots of timber for European ships and buildings. Explorers also found gold, silver, and other precious minerals here.

Fur traders sent thousands of furs back to Europe from Canada. The skins were thick and glossy and in great supply.

New Adventures

People today are curious about the world around them, and so were the early European explorers. They had no maps when they first set out, but they wondered what was on the other side of the ocean. These brave explorers wanted to see what adventures—and riches!—they might find in new countries.

"Why Explorers Came to Canada"–Think About It

1. How did European explorers first discover Canada?
2. Why did explorers need to find a new way to China?
3. What did European countries compete against each other for?
4. What is a *missionary*?
5. Why do you think the fish from Newfoundland had to be salted and dried in the sun before being shipped back to Europe?
6. How would you feel travelling across the world without a map to guide you? Explain.

The Fur Trade

Europeans began visiting Canada regularly for the fish they could catch off the country's Atlantic coast. But it was furs that they traded for with the Indigenous people that made them explore the country and brought them into contact with other Indigenous groups.

It Started with Hats

The fur trade in North America began in the 1500s. Sailors who had travelled across the Atlantic Ocean from Europe saw the furs the Indigenous people were wearing and wanted to take them back to Europe. The native people wanted the fishermen's metal tools, including knives and axes, since they were much sharper than the stone tools they used.

The furs the Indigenous people traded included deer, ermine (a type of weasel), sea otter, and skunk. But the most popular fur was beaver. That's because beaver fur was especially useful for a process called felting.

In this cloth-making method, the hairs of the fur were matted together. The fabric produced was very warm, and hats made of this beaver-wool felt were already extremely popular in Europe. Many of the hats looked like modern-day top hats.

Every rich person had to have a beaver hat, so there were few beavers left in Europe. No wonder the fishermen were excited when they saw the Indigenous people's beaver skins. The fishermen knew they could earn a lot of money when they took the furs back to Europe.

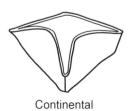

Continental

Naval

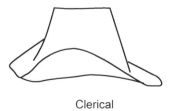

Clerical

Fashionable hats made from beaver fur were popular in 18th- and 19th-century Europe.

Exploring the Country

Fur traders from England, France, and Holland all traded with the Indigenous people. From the Maritimes, they moved up the St. Lawrence River into what is today Quebec and Ontario. In 1668, a ship sent out by England sailed into Hudson Bay and began trading with the Indigenous people living there. The Hudson's Bay Company was set up in 1670 for the fur trade and still has stores across Canada.

As the fur traders searched for more Indigenous people to trade furs with, they explored the land. But the explorers would not have survived without the Indigenous people. They knew the best trails through the woods, the fastest rivers, and how to avoid rapids.

Indigenous people also provided fur traders with food and taught them which plants were good to eat. They worked with the voyageurs, the French Canadians who transported furs by canoe—*"voyageur"* is French for "traveller." Indigenous people also traded with the coureurs des bois ("runners of the woods"), traders who travelled through the woods and less settled areas. Sometimes the European men married Indigenous women, and their children became known as the Métis.

End of the Fur Trade

As the French continued trading, they built fur-trading forts. Indigenous villages sprang up around the forts. Many of today's cities, such as Kingston, Montreal, and Toronto, are located where fur-trade forts once stood.

By the mid-1800s, the craze for beaver fur hats in Europe was over. But it changed the lives of Indigenous people forever.

"The Fur Trade"–Think About It

1. What made Europeans explore the country?
2. What did the Indigenous people want from the fishermen, and why?
3. What was the most popular fur?
4. Why were the fishermen excited when they saw the beaver skins the Indigenous people had?
5. What happened in 1670?
6. Who were the voyageurs? What does *voyageur* mean?

Indigenous Peoples of Canada © Chalkboard Publishing Inc.

Fur Trade Routes

From the early 1600s to the 1850s, Europeans explored the land now known as Canada. They were searching for Indigenous people so the two groups could trade together. The Europeans wanted animal furs, especially beaver pelts. Indigenous people traded their furs for metal tools and other items. These people who had lived on the land for thousands of years knew the best ways to move across the country and they shared their knowledge with the fur traders and explorers.

Up the St. Lawrence

In the Maritimes there is no large river system, so trade was focused on the coast of the Atlantic Ocean and the banks of the St. Lawrence River. But as traders paddled up that huge river, they realized it was connected to many other smaller rivers. These tributaries (streams that flow into larger streams or lakes) allowed the Europeans to explore what is now Ontario and Quebec.

By the 1740s, the fur traders had travelled through the Great Lakes to the "head," or far end, of Lake Superior. That allowed them to begin exploring the Prairies and trading with the Indigenous people who lived there. It took about 13 weeks for voyageurs to paddle and portage from Montreal to Thunder Bay. ("Portage" means to carry a boat or goods on land between two bodies of water.) Today you can fly between the two cities in less than two hours!

Heading West

Other explorers sailed from Europe into Hudson Bay. Many rivers flow into this huge body of water and the fur traders were guided along these tributaries by the Indigenous people of the area.

Like the traders who paddled through the Great Lakes, explorers starting at Hudson Bay followed rivers that led west into the Prairies. Eventually, fur traders trekked along mountain passes through the Rocky Mountains and along the Columbia River to the Pacific Ocean.

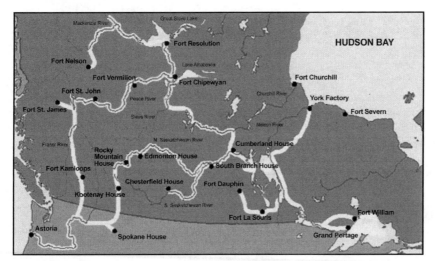

Western fur trade routes and trading posts, 1821–1870

Many rivers have rapids in various places. Rapids are places in the river where the water and current run very fast. Waterfalls, such as Niagara Falls, also couldn't be paddled through. So the fur traders had to portage, carrying on their backs their food, furs, and canoes from one area of a river that was safe enough to paddle to the next. Indigenous people knew where portaging was the only way to move forward, and they knew the shortest routes.

Trading and Exploring

Some of the routes that the fur traders explored had too many rapids and too much rough water for them to become trade routes. But even these rivers allowed Europeans to explore the country. For instance, fur trader Simon Fraser is best known today as an explorer. In 1808 he journeyed through British Columbia and the waterway now known as the Fraser River.

Today, most travel in Canada is done in cars or in planes. But in the days of the fur trade, lakes and rivers were the "highways," and the fastest way to move was in canoes. Trade routes along these rivers developed to link villages of Indigenous people who were willing to trade with the Europeans.

"Fur Trade Routes"–Think About It

1. How did the St. Lawrence River allow the Europeans to explore what is now Ontario and Quebec?
2. What allowed the fur traders to begin exploring the Prairies?
3. How did the fur traders reach the Pacific Ocean?
4. What does *portage* mean?
5. Why did the fur traders sometimes have to portage?
6. Who was Simon Fraser, and what did he do?

Peace and Friendship Treaties

A treaty is an agreement between groups of people. Indigenous people have been making treaties for thousands of years with other groups on Turtle Island (North America). These treaties helped them to work out the boundaries of territories, to trade goods, and to travel safely through the territories of other Indigenous groups.

In the Maritimes

When explorers and visitors from Europe came to Turtle Island, Indigenous people made treaties with them. These early treaties are called Peace and Friendship Treaties.

In the Maritimes, the Peace and Friendship Treaties were written down and signed between Britain and Indigenous groups such as the Maliseet, Mi'kmaq, and Passamaquoddy peoples. These groups had lived in the Maritimes and Gaspé area (today part of the province of Quebec) and the northeastern United States for thousands of years. Their first contact with non-Indigenous people was with fishermen from France, Portugal, and Spain. The Europeans began coming to the Atlantic coast in the 1500s.

But the Indigenous people didn't have a lot to do with these visitors because the fishermen spent only a short time on land. The British came to Turtle Island in the late 1500s looking for furs to ship back to England. They traded items such as beads, mirrors, and tobacco for beaver skins from Indigenous people. That meant the British spent a lot of time on the land and had many encounters with Indigenous people.

The First Peace and Friendship Treaty

The French were in Canada at the same time as the British. During the 1600s and 1700s, the countries of Britain and France fought each other for control of what is now Canada. (Canada didn't become a country until Confederation in 1867.) The French were the first to team up with the Indigenous people of the area for trading and to help them in their battles with the English.

An 1886 copy of the original 1725 Peace and Friendship Treaty.

But when France lost a war in Europe, it was also forced to give up some of its land in Canada, including areas in the Maritimes. To make trade easier and to try to promote peace there, Britain negotiated with the area's Indigenous peoples. On December 15, 1725, the two groups signed a Peace and Friendship Treaty in Boston, Massachusetts.

In this treaty, the Indigenous people didn't give up any of their rights to land or to resources, such as fish, furs, minerals, or trees. Instead, the treaty recognized that Maliseet and Mi'kmaq owned the land, and included rules for the relationship between the Indigenous peoples and the British.

The Treaties Today

Because the French kept encouraging their Indigenous allies to attack the British settlements, peace in the area didn't last long. But Indigenous peoples and Britain signed a number of Peace and Friendship Treaties between 1725 and 1779.

Peace and Friendship Treaties are different from other treaties because they don't involve an exchange of land, hunting rights, payments, or other benefits. These treaties still apply today. Canada's Constitution recognizes Peace and Friendship Treaties and the rights that they include.

"Peace and Friendship Treaties"–Think About It

1. Name three things treaties helped Indigenous peoples do.
2. What did the British give Indigenous peoples in exchange for beaver skins?
3. Why did Britain and France fight during the 1600s and 1700s?
4. What did the Peace and Friendship Treaty of 1725 do?
5. How are Peace and Friendship Treaties different from other treaties?

Samuel de Champlain

North America looked very different before Canada, the United States, and Mexico became countries. Starting in the 1500s, European explorers came to North America and claimed land for their countries. The map below shows what land these countries claimed in the early 1700s in the eastern part of North America.

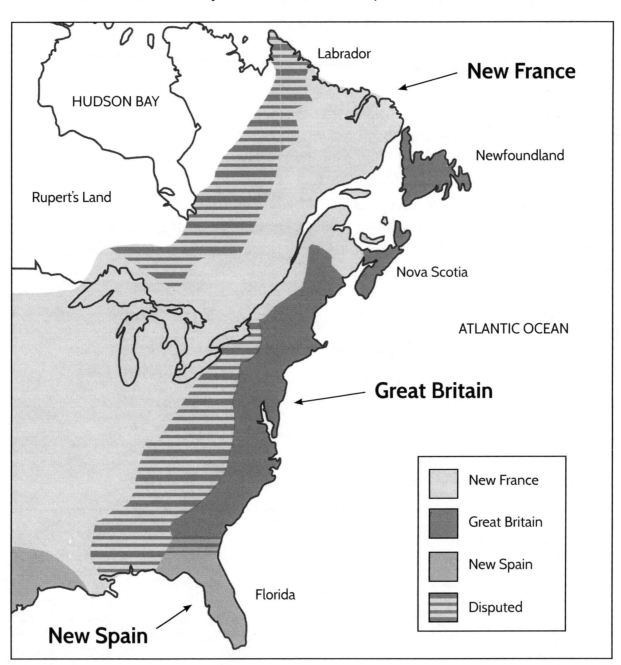

Samuel de Champlain

Samuel de Champlain is called the Father of New France. This is because he explored and mapped much of the area. He also founded colonies. Later, he governed New France. Here are some highlights of Samuel de Champlain's life and accomplishments:

- Champlain is born around 1567 in France.

- 1599–1601: Champlain is part of a voyage to explore the Caribbean.

- 1603: Champlain travels to North America as part of a fur-trading voyage. He maps the St. Lawrence River. He writes a book about his voyage when he returns to France.

- 1604: Champlain makes another trip to North America. He helps found a colony on Saint Croix Island.

- 1605: Champlain and the settlers move from Saint Croix Island to Port Royal. Champlain explores and maps the Atlantic coast down to Cape Cod. He returns to France in 1607.

- 1608: Champlain returns to New France and founds a colony that becomes Quebec City. He forms an alliance with the Huron and Algonquin. He promises to help them with their fight against their enemy—the Iroquois. He discovers (and names for himself) Lake Champlain.

- July, 1608: Champlain and his First Nations allies fight a battle with the Iroquois. Champlain and his allies win. The Iroquois become enemies of the French.

- 1612: Champlain is given powers by the French government to run New France. He continues exploring and mapping.

- 1615: Champlain is injured in an attack by the Iroquois. He spends the winter with the Huron and learns many things about how they live. He goes back to France after recovering.

- 1620: Champlain returns to New France. He does not explore anymore but spends his time governing New France.

- 1629: Quebec City is captured by the British and Champlain is sent to England as a prisoner.

- 1633: Quebec City is given back to the French and Champlain returns to New France to govern.

- 1635: Champlain dies in Quebec City.

"Samuel de Champlain"–Think About It

1. What did you learn about North America from the first paragraph? What did you learn from the map? Use your answers to write a summary of what North America was like in the 1600s.
2. What happened in 1608?
3. Find the words *alliance* and *allies* in the text. How are these words the same? How are they different?
4. Why did the French and the Iroquois become enemies? Support your answer with details from the text.
5. Champlain is called the Father of New France. What reasons does the text give for this? Include specific examples in your answer.

Fur Traders and Settlers in New France

Two groups of people who came to New France were fur traders and settlers. They came for different reasons, but both groups played an important part in the development of New France.

The Fur Traders

The fur trade was the economic start of New France. It was how people who came to New France made money. The fur traders had one goal: to get as many furs as they could. Beavers were the most important source of fur for them. Fur traders got their furs from First Nations peoples so they formed alliances, mostly with the Huron. This led to conflict later on with other First Nations and with the British. The traders also travelled farther into the continent in search of more and better furs, so they helped open up new land.

Fur traders on a river in New France.

The fur trade caused changes in the way of life of the First Nations. Before, they had lived in harmony with nature. They took from the land and the animals only what they needed. Now they hunted animals to trade for goods from the fur traders. In some areas, certain animals were endangered.

The fur traders spent much of their time living with their First Nations allies. Many married First Nations women. Their children were the first of the Métis people.

The Settlers

The French first came to North America for fish, then for furs. Then they decided to build permanent settlements to help control the areas they were in. The French wanted settlements along the St. Lawrence River and around the Great Lakes. To do this, they needed settlers. The settlers who came were mostly farmers. Many of the settlers also worked in the fur trade to make money.

In the beginning, most of the settlers were single men. The king of France decided to send women to the new settlements. From 1663 to 1673, 1,000 single women were sent. Many were orphans. They married as soon as they could and had as many children as possible. In this way, the population of New France grew. The women brought a dowry, or gift, of money from the king, and families were given extra money based on the number of children they had.

Life was hard for most of the settlers. They had to clear land, build homes, grow crops, and pay taxes. Diseases such as cholera and smallpox were common. But for most, life was better in New France than it would have been in France. By 1750, there were about 70,000 French people living along the St. Lawrence River.

"Fur Traders and Settlers in New France"–Think About It

1. What was the main reason fur traders came to New France? What was the main reason settlers came to New France? How were their lives different?
2. What did you learn about the women who were sent to New France by the king? Why do you think these women were chosen?
3. Some settlers worked in the fur trade to make money. Why do you think settlers chose to make money in this way?
4. What was the relationship between the fur traders and the First Nations?
5. What changed for the First Nations after they started to trade for furs?

Indigenous Women and the Fur Trade

Beginning in the early 1500s, Indigenous women were vital to the fur traders who came to Canada to explore the country, buy furs, and ship them back to Europe. Without the help of these women, the fur traders would not have survived.

Knowledge of the Land

Indigenous women acted as guides and interpreters for the fur traders. The women knew the cultures of the various Indigenous groups, as well as many of the languages. They could guide the Europeans through wilderness trails and along Canada's rivers and lakes.

As well, Indigenous women knew the best places to set up camp and how to prepare a campsite. They gathered firewood, lit fires, cooked meals, and knew how to make comfortable beds using furs and tree boughs.

Food for Survival

Indigenous women knew which leaves, roots, shoots, fruits, vegetables, and berries could be eaten. They knew how to fish and how to trap animals for food, and how to turn them into delicious meals over a campfire.

Indigenous women also knew how to preserve food so that it could be eaten throughout the long, cold winters, when fresh food was hard to find. They dried berries and other fruits in the sun or over a fire. The women also ground corn into meal that they could store and use for making bread when needed.

Pemmican is an Indigenous food that fur traders especially liked. A mixture of dried meat, fat, and dried berries, it is high in protein and lasts a long time. No wonder many Indigenous people still make it today. Indigenous women also made a flatbread called *bannock* that is still popular today, and some made a corn stew known as *sagamit*.

An Algonquin woman stretches a deer hide.

Preparing Furs

Fur traders depended on Indigenous women to clean and prepare furs so they could be sent to Europe, where they would be sold for high prices. The women knew where to find the animals with the best skins, and how to trap the animals. The women also knew how to scrape, stretch, and dry the skins.

"Indigenous Women and the Fur Trade"–Think About It!

1. How did Indigenous women's knowledge help the fur traders?
   List two examples for each area.

Knowledge of the Land	
Food for Survival	
Preparing Furs	

2. Using information from the text and your own ideas, why were Indigenous women vital to the fur trade?

3. Why was it important that the Indigenous women knew how to preserve food?

4. Describe each of the following: a) pemmican b) sagamit c) bannock.

5. Aside from making stew with it, how did Indigenous women use corn?

Indigenous Peoples of Canada © Chalkboard Publishing Inc.

Explorers Depended on Indigenous People

Indigenous people in Canada shared their knowledge of the land and their inventions with the early explorers and settlers to help them survive.

Eating Well and Staying Healthy

There were many plants in Canada that the Europeans had never seen before. Indigenous people taught the newcomers which berries, roots, and fruit were safe to eat, and which were poisonous. Indigenous people also showed explorers how to trap Canada's animals for food and furs.

Indigenous women were skilled at preparing a number of foods that were very nutritious, such as pemmican and bannock (also called "trail bread" or "bush bread"), which the explorers could easily carry with them.

Indigenous people made medicines from the plants around them. In winter, early settlers often suffered from scurvy, which is a disease caused by not getting enough vitamin C. Indigenous people taught the Europeans how to make a tea from cedar bark and leaves. The tea was full of vitamin C and helped save the settlers' lives.

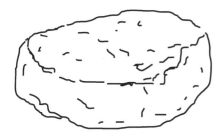

pemmican

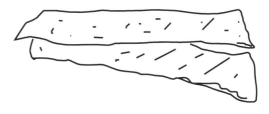

bannock

Getting Around

Indigenous peoples invented canoes, snowshoes, and sleds to get around in Canada. Explorers and settlers quickly realized how useful these inventions were, and the Indigenous peoples taught the Europeans how to use them.

When the explorers first came to Canada, there were no maps for them to make their way through the wilderness. Indigenous men acted as guides. They showed the Europeans the best land trails and water routes for travelling across this vast country. The Indigenous men drew maps on birchbark, on the ground, or in the snow.

Surviving the Cold

Winters in Canada were longer and colder than the Europeans had ever experienced. The First Nations and the Inuit taught the explorers and settlers how to survive here. Indigenous women sewed fur coats, leggings, and mittens for the Europeans.

"Explorers Depended on Indigenous Peoples"–Think About It

1. List ways Indigenous peoples helped Canada's early explorers in each of these areas.

Eating well and staying healthy	
Getting around	
Surviving the cold	

2. Imagine you are an early European explorer experiencing your first winter in Canada. Write a journal entry telling what winter is like, and how Indigenous people helped you and your fellow explorers.

3. What is *scurvy* and how was it cured by the Indigenous people?

4. How did Indigenous women help the Europeans survive the winter?

The Indian Act

The Indian Act is a group of laws the Canadian government passed in 1876. It is still the law today. The laws set out how the government works with the country's more than 600 First Nations. But the Canadian government passed these laws without any input or agreement from First Nations, and the Indian Act continues to cause problems today.

Why Is It Still Called the Indian Act?

The name "Indian" is a term used in old laws and documents. Today it is more correct to use the term First Nations. But some First Nations chiefs think that changing the name "Indian Act" is a bad idea. They worry that it could change their legal relationship with the government of Canada. The Indian Act applies only to First Nations, not to the Métis or Inuit.

The Purpose of the Indian Act

The Indian Act had three purposes. One was to decide who could have "Indian" status, which means the person could be described as belonging to a First Nation.

Another purpose of the Indian Act was to assimilate, or absorb, the First Nations into Canadian society. The act didn't accept the First Nations system of clans or kinship. Instead, it said only immediate family could belong to a specific band. That made it difficult for members of First Nations to stay in touch with their large extended families.

The last purpose of the Indian Act was to set out which land the First Nations could use. It promised them reserves on good, fertile land. However, as more Europeans came to Canada and wanted to settle there, the government needed more land and found ways to take it away from the First Nations.

According to the Indian Act, First Nations don't own the land where their reserves are located. The Canadian government holds the land in trust, which means the government doesn't own it but is responsible for all decisions that are made about it.

Changes to the Act

Since the Indian Act became law more than 140 years ago, it has been amended, or changed, 42 times. For instance, in 1885 a ban on the potlatch was added. This gift-giving ceremony is very important to west coast First Nations peoples for building connections in the community.

But the Canadian government saw the potlatch as non-European and banned it, trying to assimilate the First Nations. It wasn't until 1951 that the potlatch was made legal again.

Thanks to another change to the Indian Act, in 1960, people who don't have Indigenous status can finally live on First Nations reserves with their families.

The Indian Act Today

The Indian Act affects the way First Nations bands and reserves can spend their money and operate. Now First Nations peoples want to replace the act with laws that respect treaties made between the government and First Nations.

"The Indian Act"–Think About It

1. What does the Indian Act aim to do?
2. What are the three purposes of the Indian Act?
3. Which Indigenous peoples does the Indian Act apply to?
4. What is a *potlach*? Why is it important to west coast First Nations?
5. Why do you think the Indian Act still causes problems today?
6. A change was made to the Indian Act in 1960. What does this change mean for people who don't have Indigenous status? Using your own ideas, explain why this change would be important to families.

First Nations Reserves

Land that has been set apart by the government for a First Nations band to use is called a reserve. There are more than 3,100 reserves across Canada. These lands are known as reservations in the United States but in Canada they are called reserves.

Reserves Across Canada

More than 360,000 people live on reserves across the country—that's almost half of all Canada's First Nations. The Inuit and Métis don't usually live on reserves. However, many live in communities that were set up based on land claims, or have some other agreement with Canada's government to govern themselves.

Reserves range in size from about 13,000 people to fewer than 500. Some reserves are so small and remote that no one lives there. They're used only occasionally, such as for trapping and similar activities.

Canada's largest reserve is the Kainai (Blood) First Nations reserve, in southwestern Alberta. It has one of the highest populations of any reserve. The reserves with the largest populations are the Six Nations of the Grand River reserve, near Brantford in southwestern Ontario, and the Mohawks of Akwesasne reserve, in southeastern Ontario near Cornwall.

Problems on Reserves

Many reserves in Canada are in remote countryside. This means it can be hard for First Nations living there to find jobs, since there are few businesses nearby. Many people on reserves live in poverty. As well, services such as hospital care and education may be more limited than in towns and cities. A lot of reserves have water that is not safe to drink.

First Nations groups are now working to make changes so reserves can become good places to live, with jobs for the people living there. For First Nations, reserves are not just a physical home, but a spiritual one.

Urban Reserves

Since the early 1980s, First Nations have been creating urban reserves. These are First Nations communities that are in or near towns and cities. Some urban reserves were rural when they were first set up but became urban as towns grew around them. First Nations were able to create urban reserves thanks to land claim settlements. These payments from the Canadian and provincial governments have allowed First Nations to buy land.

Today, there are more than 120 urban reserves across the country. The first one was set up by the Fishing Lake First Nation in 1981 at Kylemore in southeastern Saskatchewan. Some urban reserves are in large cities, such as Vancouver, while others are in smaller centres like Portage la Prairie in Manitoba.

Just south of Saskatoon, Saskatchewan, the English River First Nation runs the Grasswood Travel and Business Centre. The offices and stores there have created jobs and new businesses. The First Nations University of Canada is located on an urban reserve in Regina, Saskatchewan. It is Canada's first university on a reserve.

The Huron-Wendat First Nation built its urban reserve at Wendake, near Quebec City, into an important cultural and tourism centre. Many festivals and powwows are held here each year.

"First Nations Reserves"–Think About It

1. What is a *reserve*?
2. What are some of the problems First Nations face on reserves?
3. Name two reserves in Canada with the largest populations.
4. How were First Nations able to create urban reserves?
5. Who set up Canada's first urban reserve? Where is it?
6. What is the name of Canada's first university on a reserve? Where is it?

Residential Schools

To force Indigenous people to assimilate into the culture of Canada's settlers, residential schools were set up for Indigenous children. These schools got this name because the children had to live in them—that is, make their residence there.

Losing their Culture

The first residential schools opened in the 1880s. The Canadian government believed that if Indigenous children were schooled by non-Indigenous teachers, they would forget about their customs, families, language, and Indigenous past.

Children as young as six years were taken from their families and put into the care of strangers at the schools. When the children first arrived, their long hair was cut off to make them look less Indigenous. As well, their names were changed to make them sound more "Canadian" and to separate them from their families. If the children spoke their Indigenous languages they were punished, sometimes beaten.

The teachers and school officials abused the children mentally, physically, and sexually. The children were rarely allowed to visit their families, and visits from relatives were discouraged. The children were terribly lonely and longed for home.

The Effects of Residential Schools

Although Indigenous parents were told their children would receive a good education at residential schools, they actually were taught very little. Instead, they spent most of their time doing jobs such as cleaning, sweeping, and dusting. Meanwhile, they were missing out on learning traditional Indigenous skills, such as hunting, fishing, and trapping.

About 150,000 Indigenous children were forced to attend residential schools during the 150 years that they operated. That's almost one-third of the country's Indigenous people. The conditions were so bad that more than 6,000 children died while in the schools. The children who did return home were very damaged by the experience and found it difficult to fit into the traditional cultures of their home communities.

They had grown up without parents and were cared for by strangers, and so didn't know how to be parents themselves when they were older.

By the mid-1970s, most residential schools across the country had been closed. The last one, which was located in Saskatchewan, closed in 1996. But the pain the schools had caused has still not gone away.

The Truth and Reconciliation Commission

In June 2008, the Truth and Reconciliation Commission was set up to look into the abuse caused by the residential schools. At this time, Prime Minister Stephen Harper offered a full apology on behalf of Canadians for the Indian Residential Schools system. The commission aimed to help find healing for the Indigenous people who were affected. Events were held across the country to give people who had attended residential schools a chance to tell their stories. These meetings also let others hear what they had gone through and the effect this abuse was still having on them.

The Truth and Reconciliation Commission was completed in December 2015 and the documents from the hearings are now at the National Centre for Truth and Reconciliation in Winnipeg, Manitoba. The commission was created in the belief that it is important Canadians not forget what they learned about how Indigenous people suffered because of the residential schools, and that Canada needs to find ways to support Indigenous people as they heal from the destruction these schools caused.

"Residential Schools"–Think About It

1. Why were residential schools set up for Indigenous children?
2. What did the Canadian government believe would happen if Indigenous children were schooled by non-Indigenous teachers?
3. Name two things that happened to Indigenous children when they went to the residential schools.
4. What were some of the effects of the residential schools on the children who returned home?
5. What was the Truth and Reconciliation Commission set up to do?
6. Using information from the text and your own ideas, how do you think Indigenous children and their families felt about residential schools?

Land Claims

Long ago, when settlers came to what is now called Canada, the government moved many First Nations from the lands where they had lived for thousands of years. The government signed treaties with First Nations to allow settlers to create settlements on First Nations land. These treaties outlined how the two groups would live on the land.

However, the government didn't always give the First Nations all the land that the treaties promised. So, for many decades they have had to negotiate with the Canadian government either to get back their original land or to receive land somewhere else. These negotiations are known as land claims.

Types of Land Claims

There are three types of land claims made by First Nations. "Specific claims" are based on treaties, or agreements, from the past that were made between First Nations and the Canadian government.

"Comprehensive claims" are about First Nations land rights that haven't already been covered in historic treaties. Because of this, these land claims are sometimes called modern treaties. This type of land claim is always about land.

"Treaty entitlement land claims" are made when First Nations don't receive all the land they're entitled to according to a treaty. In settlement of these types of claims, First Nations may be given money, or they may receive Crown land (land that is owned by the federal or provincial government).

Land Claim Settlements

The Osoyoos band in British Columbia was angry because in 1877 it was relocated to an area much smaller than it had been promised. The money it received in the 1990s has allowed it to develop businesses, so there is almost no unemployment on the reserve.

In 1907, the Canadian government moved the Peguis First Nation from their land in southeastern Manitoba to land farther north that was very swampy. The band began negotiating with the government in 1998 to receive compensation for the move. When Canada agreed that the land had been taken illegally, the Peguis received money that they used to build homes and invest in the band's future.

The Chapleau Cree First Nation signed a land treaty with the government in 1905 but never received the amount of land it should have. So, in 2016 this First Nation negotiated a settlement with the Canadian and Ontario governments that gave them money from the federal government and land from the provincial government.

Settling land claims helps a lot to improve relations between First Nations and non-Indigenous people in Canada.

Nunavut

To settle a land claim by the Inuit people, the territory of Nunavut was formed in 1999. It was created because many Inuit wanted land where they could make decisions for themselves.

There were years of negotiations and votes by the Canadian government and the Inuit. Finally, the new territory was created from a portion of the Northwest Territories. The name Nunavut means "our land" in Inuktitut. It's the country's largest territory, and covers about one-fifth of Canada.

"Land Claims"–Think About It

1. Why did the Canadian government sign treaties with First Nations?
2. What did the treaties do?
3. Why have some First Nations had to negotiate with the Canadian government?
4. Which type of land claim is sometimes called a modern treaty? Why?
5. Name two First Nations that successfully negotiated land claim settlements.
6. Why was the territory of Nunavut formed?

What is a Powwow?

Frequently during the summer months Indigenous people come together to celebrate their traditions through singing, dancing, eating, and the selling of handmade arts and crafts. These festive occasions are called *powwows*.

At powwows, members of Indigenous nations get to meet up with old friends (and make new ones), offer news and support for their communities, eat traditional Indigenous food, and teach their children about Indigenous culture in an entertaining and memorable way.

Powwows are held on reserves and in cities across Canada, usually on summer weekends. Sometimes non-Indigenous people can attend a powwow and take part in some of the dances, which is a great way to learn about Indigenous culture.

Powwows might have different songs, dances, food, or crafts, depending on which Indigenous group is hosting, but a powwow always has dancing, drumming, and singing. The dancers are dressed in elaborate, beautifully coloured clothing. This special clothing, along with specially made moccasins, fans, headdresses, and jewellery, are called *regalia*. Singing, dancing, drumming, and regalia are sacred elements of a powwow. As well as entertaining, they tell important stories about Indigenous culture.

A powwow always has music. Here, male musicians play and sing in a Drum Circle. Dancers perform to the music.

Women perform a Fancy Shawl dance.

Men and women dance separately, and have different dances. For instance, men's dances include the Grass dance and the Fancy dance, and women's include the Jingle Dress dance and the Fancy Shawl dance. Kids can dance too—in fact, at some powwows, kids can compete in categories that are just for them.

There are two main types of powwows: competitive and traditional. At competitive powwows, dancers and musicians compete for prizes. But both kinds of powwows foster pride among Indigenous peoples, and help them keep their traditions alive. Because a main function of powwows is to encourage a sense of cultural pride and respect, alcohol and drugs are not allowed on powwow grounds.

We don't know for sure where the word powwow comes from. Some say it comes from *pa wa*, meaning "to eat" in the language of the Pawnee, an American tribe. Others believe it comes from the Algonquin words *pau wau*, which means "he who dreams." The Europeans who came to the New World changed it to the word we use now: powwow.

"What is a Powwow?"—Think About It

1. Why do Indigenous people come together at a powwow?
2. What are three things that always take place at a powwow?
3. What are *regalia?*
4. What are the sacred elements of a powwow?
5. What are the two main types of powwow?
6. Would you like to attend a powwow? Why or why not?

Indigenous Symbols Today

Thousands of years ago, Indigenous people created petroglyphs (designs carved into stone), pictographs (pictures painted on rock walls), Inuksuit (Inuit stone figures marking important locations), and many other important designs and symbols. Today's Indigenous people have many more symbols.

Flying Proudly

Nunavut officially separated from the Northwest Territories in 1999, making it Canada's largest and most northerly territory. The flag that was designed for the new territory shows the North Star in vivid blue on a white background, and a red Inukshuk with golden yellow on its left. The bright colours symbolize Nunavut's wealth.

The Nunavut flag

First Nations also create flags to commemorate important events in their histories. For instance, Treaty 4 was an agreement between Britain and a number of First Nations governments. It covers most of modern-day southern Saskatchewan and was signed in 1874. About 100 years later, an elder designed a flag representing the treaty. It includes a medicine wheel symbolizing land, sky, and water.

Treaty 6 covers much of the central part of what is today Saskatchewan and Alberta. The British government signed it with First Nations leaders in 1876. The flag symbolizing this treaty shows the British flag behind a Treaty 6 medal. The sun, grass, and water on the medal symbolize the treaty's endurance for "as long as the sun shines, the grass grows and the water flows."

Métis Symbols

The Métis have a flag to represent their culture. In the middle is a white infinity symbol—it looks like a figure eight on its side. This symbol represents both the Indigenous and European peoples that came together to make one unique culture.

The Metis flag

Sometimes the Métis flag has a red background and sometimes it has a blue one. The blue flag represents Métis who worked for the North West Company in the fur trade. The red flag is for Métis employed by the Hudson's Bay Company (which still has stores across the country). Today, the blue flag is the flag of the Métis Nation across Canada, while the red flag is for the Métis Nation of Alberta.

Another Métis symbol is the *ceinture fléchée*, or "arrow sash." It was very popular during fur-trade days and gets its name from its woven designs and patterns. The sash kept its wearer warm, but could also be used as a sling, a rope, and more.

Orange Shirt Day

Modern clothes can be symbols too. On September 30 each year, many Indigenous and non-Indigenous people wear orange shirts. This is to remind Canadians of Phyllis Webstad. In 1973, six-year-old Phyllis was taken from her First Nations family in Williams Lake, British Columbia, and sent to a residential school, where she and the other First Nations children were not allowed to speak their native languages and had to give up their culture.

Every Child Matters button

On Phyllis's first day at residential school, her brand new orange shirt was taken from her. Launched in 2013, Orange Shirt Day reminds people of the many First Nations children who were forced to attend residential schools.

The Canadian Inuit Dog

The Inuit had a special kind of dog to pull their sleds. The Canadian Inuit Dog is a purebred working dog. It can pull twice its weight, even over rough land or ice in freezing winter weather. The dogs also helped the Inuit hunt by sniffing out seal breathing holes in the sea ice. They also helped hunt musk oxen, and sometimes even kept polar bears from attacking. In recognition of this special breed, the government of Nunavut made the Canadian Inuit Dog the territory's official animal.

In 1997, the Royal Canadian Mint issued a sterling silver coin honouring some of Canada's favourite canine companions, including the Canadian Inuit Dog.

Inukshuk

Because the Arctic can seem like a bleak place, filled with nothing but snow and rocks, the Inuit built stone figures called Inuksuit (pronounced *Ee-nook-shoo-eet*) to help guide travellers. A single one of these figures is called an Inuksuk (pronounced *Ee-nook-shook*). Inuksuk means "in the shape of a human." Inuksuit were made from boulders or stones, and were placed all over the landscape. They pointed the way, showed where someone had gone so that others could follow, or marked a place where food was hidden. Some of these incredible stone figures are believed to be thousands of years old.

Inukshuk landmark in Rankin Inlet, Nunavut

"Indigenous Symbols Today"–Think About It

1. What are the four colours of Nunavut's flag, and what do they mean?
2. What do the sun, grass, and water on the Treaty 6 medal stand for?
3. What is an *infinity symbol,* and what does it represent?
4. When is Orange Shirt Day? What is its purpose?
5. Name some of the purposes of the Inukshuk.

Traditional Ecological Knowledge

For thousands of years, Indigenous peoples have studied and learned about their environments. Today, this awareness is called Traditional Ecological Knowledge (TEK). It refers to the way Indigenous peoples interact with plants and other animals in the natural world, and how their knowledge guides non-Indigenous scientists today.

The Exxon Valdez oil tanker, which hit a reef off Alaska in 1989.

Non-Indigenous scientists also use TEK to help wildlife. During the cleanup following the oil spill by the Exxon Valdez tanker in 1989, Indigenous people shared TEK about conditions before the spill. The native people knew a lot about the animals that had been hurt by the spill, such as how many lived in the area, where they lived, and what they ate. By combining scientific data and TEK, as well as asking the Indigenous communities for assistance cleaning up, scientists helped many more animals.

A bird covered in oil from an oil spill

TEK has also helped scientists learn more about climate change. For instance, it has provided a lot of information about the polar bear and how its environment is threatened. There are fewer and fewer polar bears, and TEK informs scientists about their diet, where they live, and how their population is changing as their territories are altered.

Polar bears in the Canadian Artic

"Tradition Ecological Knowledge"—Think About It

Using information from the text and your own ideas, create an informational poster about TEK.

Create a Magazine

Congratulations!
Your class has been selected to create a new magazine to share information about Indigenous Peoples of Canada.

The various groups of Indigenous people in Canada each had their own culture—myths and legends, ways of travel, the food they ate and how they obtained it, the types of dwellings they lived in and the ways in which they travelled. Many aspects of their cultures still influence life today. For example:

- Did you know that Indigenous people discovered the first chewing gum, which was collected from spruce trees?
- Did you know that Indigenous people created the game of lawn darts, adding feathers to cobs of new green corn that had had their kernels removed?
- Did you know that many cough syrups today use the same ingredient found in pine bark that Indigenous people used?
- Did you know that corn, which is a staple food that is grown around the world, was cultivated by Indigenous people for thousands of years?

Step One: Let's Get Started!

Have each member of your group choose one of the Indigenous cultures below to write a section in the magazine.

- Peoples of the Northwest Coast
- Peoples of the Plains
- Hunters or Farmers of the Eastern Woodlands
- Peoples of the Plateau
- Other _____
- Peoples of the Arctic

List your group members:

_____

_____

Step Two: Become an Expert Historian!

Usually, historians look at four categories of information when learning about a culture. Use the chart below to help organize your section on an Indigenous culture into four parts. Make to sure to include all topics for each area in your section.

Environment

How did the surrounding air, land, and water influence the Indigenous culture?

Article Topics:
- ☐ climate
- ☐ vegetation
- ☐ natural resources
- ☐ bodies of water

Social Life

How did people in each Indigenous group relate to each other?

Article Topics:
- ☐ social structure
- ☐ family
- ☐ education
- ☐ spiritual beliefs
- ☐ arts
- ☐ recreation

Political Life

How did Indigenous people make decisions as a group?

Article Topics:
- ☐ political structure
- ☐ defence and war
- ☐ government

Economic Life

How did Indigenous people meet their physical needs in order to survive?

Article Topics:
- ☐ food and hunting or farming
- ☐ dwellings
- ☐ trade
- ☐ transportation
- ☐ health
- ☐ clothing

Step Three: More Magazine Ideas

Article ideas and columns to include in your magazine:

- Biography of an inspirational Indigenous person
- An interview with an Indigenous elder
- Advertisements of Indigenous community events

- Important contributions by Indigenous people
- Retelling of a myth or legend
- A profile of a reserve

Step Four: Magazine Checklist

Here is a checklist for a top-quality magazine:

Magazine Cover
- ☐ The title of the magazine is easy to read and prominent on the cover.
- ☐ There is an attractive illustration to let readers know the theme of the magazine.
- ☐ There are one or two highlight statements about what is inside the magazine.

Editor's Page
- ☐ The letter is addressed to the readers.
- ☐ The letter lets readers know why you think it is important to study Indigenous peoples across Canada.

Table of Contents
- ☐ There is a complete listing of what is in the magazine.

Advertisements
- ☐ There are student-created advertisements throughout the magazine, such as for modern-day items and community events that relate to the Indigenous peoples.

Magazine Articles
- ☐ A detailed overview of each Indigenous group
- ☐ Additional articles
- ☐ Special feature columns

Visual Appeal
- ☐ The magazine has neat and colourful pictures, maps, and other labelled diagrams.

Indigenous Artists

FAYE HEAVYSHIELD

Faye HeavyShield is a sculptor and installation artist. A member of the Kanai Nation, or Blood Tribe, she was born in 1953 on the Stand Off Reserve in Alberta, the third youngest of 12 children. As a young girl she was taken to a residential school, and in 1986 graduated from the University of Calgary. HeavyShield says her art reflects the southern Alberta landscape where she grew up, "with its prairie grass, river coulees, and wind." In her sculpture, HeavyShield depicts her childhood on the reserve, her connection to her community, her ancestry, and the natural environment.

Sculpture

Materials:
- ☐ Examples of HeavyShield's art
- ☐ Collection of common articles (buttons, clothes pegs, crayons, etc.)
- ☐ White glue
- ☐ Newsprint (or paper towels or toilet paper)
- ☐ Water
- ☐ Spray paint or acrylic paint
- ☐ Paintbrushes
- ☐ Masking tape

What to Do:
1. Demonstrate how to use the masking tape to join the common articles together to form a sculpture.
2. Explain how to mix equal parts white glue and water.
3. Add shredded newsprint (or other paper) to the water and glue to form a modelling compound.
4. Demonstrate how to apply modelling compound over the sculpture, covering the masking tape and shaping the sculpture, until satisfied with the creation.
5. Let the sculpture dry completely before applying paint.

ROBERT BOYER

Bob Boyer was a Métis Cree artist born near Prince Albert, Saskatchewan, in 1948. He was known for his politically charged paintings. Boyer used all sorts of materials in his work, such as acrylics, paper, and canvas, but he is best known for his "blanket statements"—large oil paintings on blankets. The idea to use blankets to paint on came from a trip Boyer took to Asia, where he saw paintings on silk and other cloth. The designs on these paintings were inspired by the traditional motifs of Siouan and Cree peoples in Western Canada. Some say that by using blankets, Boyer was making a statement about how Indigenous people had been treated. (In the late 1700s, it is believed, the British distributed blankets infected with smallpox, which killed thousands of Indigenous people.) Bob Boyer died in 2004.

Painting on Fabric

Materials:
- ☐ Examples of Boyer's art
- ☐ Scrap fabric (if fabric is not available, brown lunch bags may be substituted)
- ☐ Paint, permanent markers
- ☐ Geometric templates (these may be made from cardboard)
- ☐ Brushes
- ☐ Water
- ☐ Masking tape

What to Do:
1. Demonstrate how to trace geometric designs on a scrap of fabric using the permanent markers.
2. Using the masking tape, secure the fabric on all sides to a hard surface, such as a table or easel. (If using a table, a pad of newspaper slightly smaller than the fabric should be secured to the table to absorb paint that might bleed through.)
3. Carefully paint in the geometric designs and allow to dry.

NORVAL MORRISSEAU

Norval Morrisseau was a self-taught artist of Ojibway ancestry famous for his brightly coloured paintings depicting traditional Indigenous stories, spiritual themes, and political messages. Born in 1932 near Thunder Bay, Ontario, Copper Thunderbird (as Morrisseau was also known) originated the pictographic style, meaning it is like the images Indigenous peoples painted on rock walls. This style is also called "X-ray art" because it focuses on the spiritual images, or "X-rays," of the subject's feelings—their "insides." Many Indigenous artists imitated Morrisseau's style in their own work. Morrisseau, who died in 2007, is considered by many to be the grandfather of contemporary Indigenous art in Canada.

X-Ray Painting

Materials:

☐ Examples of Morrisseau's art
☐ Paint, oil pastels, crayons, or markers
☐ Pictures of animals to use as inspiration
☐ Large sheets of heavy paper
☐ Paintbrushes and water

What to Do:

1. Show students samples of Norval Morrisseau's art and share his life story. Point out how he used what is referred to as an X-Ray technique when he painted a work of art.
2. Explain that the purpose of the X-Ray technique is not only to paint the outside of a subject, but also to show the emotion and energy within the subject.
3. Instruct students to choose a subject for their painting—a fish, a bird, etc.
4. Next, have students sketch the outline of their subject on paper. Use pictures or simple outline drawings of animals for inspiration.
5. Then, students should think about the inside of their subject—their energy and emotions. What colours will they use to represent energy and emotions? What symbols will they use, and what do they mean?
6. Students can then draw lines, colours, and shapes inside the subject to represent the subject's energy and emotions. Encourage students to use their imagination.
7. You may also wish to have students write a paragraph about their artwork.

Biography Brochure

Choose an Indigenous person whom you find inspiring and would like to know more about. Use this checklist to gather research to write a biography. Make sure to explain in your biography why you chose this person.

STEP 1: Plan Your Brochure

☐ Fold a piece of paper the same way your brochure will be folded. Before writing the brochure, plan the layout in pencil. Sections of the brochure might include:
  - Why you chose this person to write about
  - Description of early life
  - Character traits
  - How he/she influenced others
  - Interesting facts
☐ Write the heading for each section where you would like it to be in the brochure.
☐ Plan where graphics or pictures will be placed in the brochure.

STEP 2: Complete a Draft

☐ Research information for each section of your brochure. Check your facts.
☐ Read your draft for meaning, then add, delete, or change words to make your writing better.
☐ Plan what illustrations or graphics you will put into your brochure.

STEP 3: Checklist

☐ My brochure is neat and well organized.
☐ My brochure has accurate information.
☐ My brochure has pictures or graphics that go well with the information.
☐ I checked the spelling.
☐ I checked the punctuation.
☐ My brochure is attractive.

Make a Collage

Choose a topic related to Indigenous people. Find pictures or words from magazines, newspapers, or other sources about your topic. Cut and paste them into a collage. On a separate piece of paper write a description of your collage.

Graphic Organizers

Graphic organizers are excellent tools to use to identify and organize information from a text into an easy-to-understand visual format. Students will expand their comprehension of a text as they complete the graphic organizers. Use these graphic organizers in addition to the activities in this book.

Concept Web – Helps students understand the main idea of a text and how it is supported by key details.

Concept Map – Helps students gain a better understanding of how different subtopics within a text connect to the topic as a whole.

Venn Diagram/Comparison Chart – Helps students focus on the comparison of two items, such as individuals, ideas, events, or pieces of information. Students can compare by looking at which things are the same, or contrast by looking at which things are different.

Fact or Opinion – Helps students to distinguish between statements of fact and opinion. Facts are pieces of information that can be proven to be true. Opinions are views or beliefs a person has, which cannot necessarily be proven to be true.

Cause and Effect – Helps students to recognize and explain relationships between events. The cause is the reason an event happens and the effect is the event that happens.

Making Connections with What I Have Read – Helps students to connect something they have read, or experienced, with the world around them.

A Concept Web About...

_____

A **main idea** is what the text is mostly about. A **detail** is important information that tells more about the main idea.

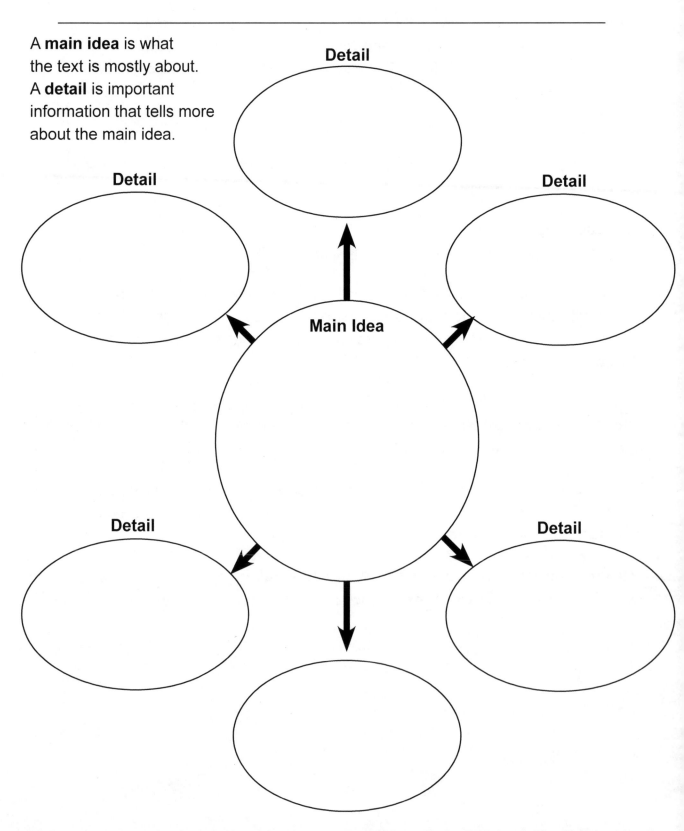

Detail

Detail

Detail

Main Idea

Detail

Detail

Concept Map

A **main idea** is what the text is mostly about.

A **subheading** is the title given to a part of a text.

A **detail** is important information that tells more about the main idea.

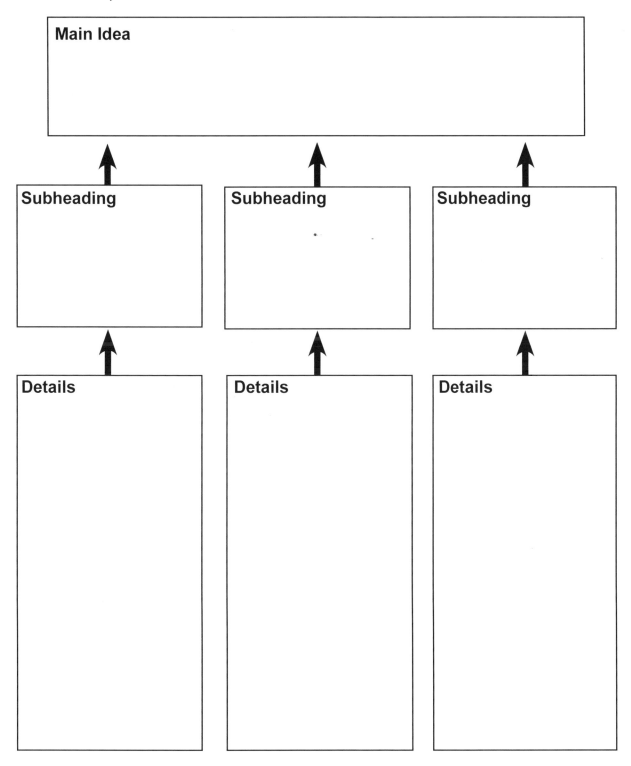

Main Idea

Subheading

Subheading

Subheading

Details

Details

Details

A Venn Diagram About...

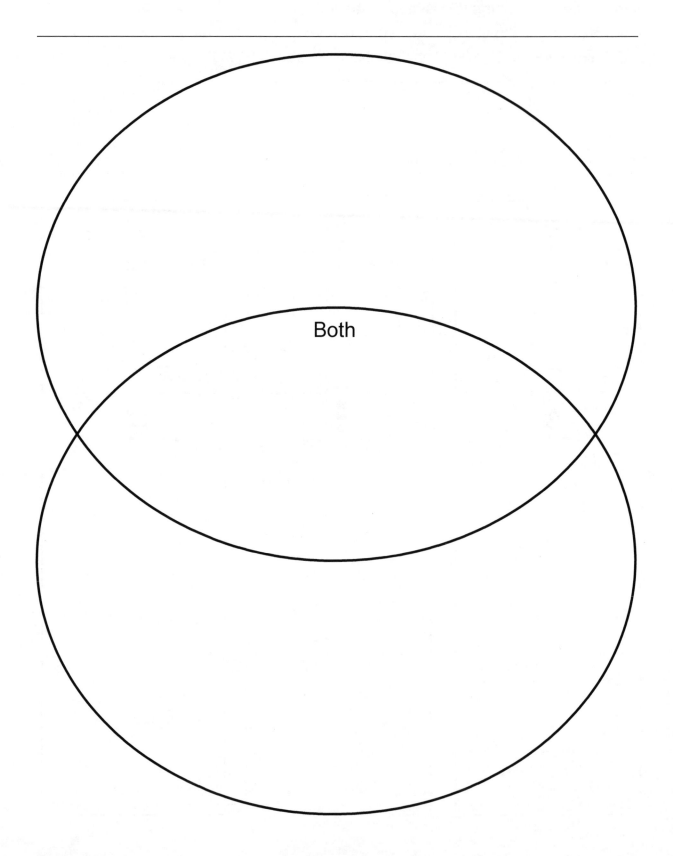

Both

A Comparison Chart

_____   (Compared with)   _____

Detailed information   **Detailed information**

Fact or Opinion

Facts: Information that can be proven to be true

Opinions: Views or beliefs a person has

Piece of Information	Fact or Opinion?	How do you know?

Cause and Effect

The **cause** is the reason something happens.

The **effect** is what happens.

Cause

Effect

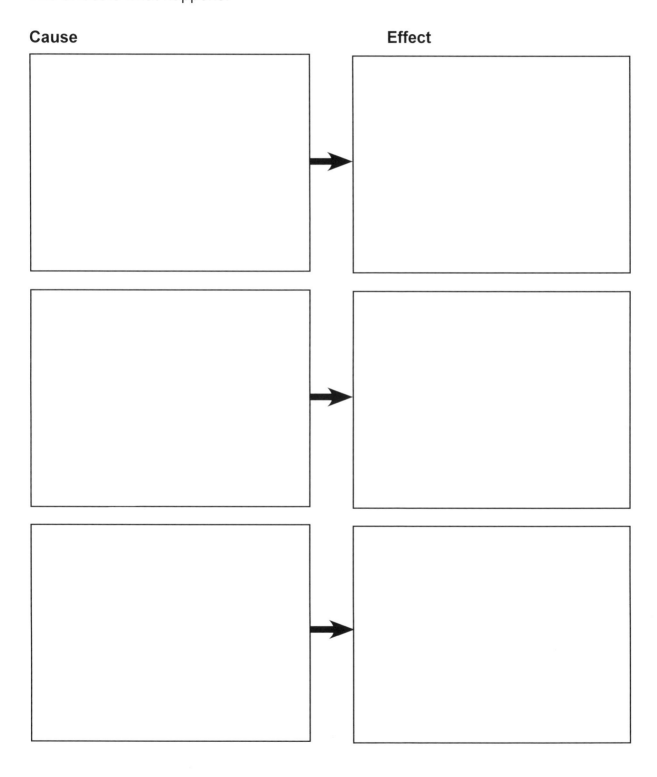

Making Connections with What I Have Read

After reading…	It reminds me of…	This helps me make a connection to…
		☐ something else I have read ☐ myself ☐ the world around me
		☐ something else I have read ☐ myself ☐ the world around me
		☐ something else I have read ☐ myself ☐ the world around me
		☐ something else I have read ☐ myself ☐ the world around me

Indigenous Peoples of Canada © Chalkboard Publishing Inc.

Student Participation Rubric

Level	Student Participation Descriptor
4	Student consistently contributes to class discussions and activities by offering ideas and asking questions.
3	Student usually contributes to class discussions and activities by offering ideas and asking questions.
2	Student sometimes contributes to class discussions and activities by offering ideas and asking questions.
1	Student rarely contributes to class discussions or activities by offering ideas or asking questions.

Understanding of Concepts Rubric

Level	Understanding of Concepts Descriptor
4	Student shows a thorough understanding of all or almost all concepts and consistently gives appropriate and complete explanations independently. No teacher support is needed.
3	Student shows a good understanding of most concepts and usually gives complete or nearly complete explanations. Infrequent teacher support is needed.
2	Student shows a satisfactory understanding of most concepts and sometimes gives appropriate, but incomplete, explanations. Teacher support is sometimes needed.
1	Student shows little understanding of concepts and rarely gives complete explanations. Intensive teacher support is needed.

Communication of Concepts Rubric

Level	Communication of Concepts Descriptor
4	Student consistently communicates with clarity and precision in written and oral work. Student consistently uses appropriate terminology and vocabulary.
3	Student usually communicates with clarity and precision in written and oral work. Student usually uses appropriate terminology and vocabulary.
2	Student sometimes communicates with clarity and precision in written and oral work. Student sometimes uses appropriate terminology and vocabulary.
1	Student rarely communicates with clarity or precision in written or oral work. Student rarely uses appropriate terminology or vocabulary.

Additional Resources

BOOKS

Arctic Stories
Michael Kusugak
Illustrated by Vladyana Langer Krykorka
Annick Press 1998
Recommended for ages 5 to 9

Acclaimed Inuit storyteller Michael Kusugak weaves a tapestry of tales about ten-year-old Agatha and her accidental heroism in the high Arctic of 1958.

A Day with Yayah
Nicola I. Campbell
Illustrated by Julie Flett
Tradewind Books 2018
Recommended for ages 4 to 7

In this story, set in British Columbia's Okanagan region, a First Nations grandmother passes down her knowledge of plant life to her young grandchildren on a family outing to forage for herbs and mushrooms.

The Diamond Willow Walking Stick: A Traditional Métis Story About Generosity
Leah Marie Dorion
Translated by Norman Fleury
Gabriel Dumont Institute 2012
Recommended for grades 4 to 7

The story explores a Métis elder's remembrances of traditional teachings about generosity that were taught to him by his grandparents. Text is in English and Michif. Included CD has both English and Michif narration of the text.

The Elders Are Watching
David Bouchard
Illustrated by Roy Henry Vickers
Raincoast Books 1997
Recommended for all ages

With gorgeous artwork and lyrical storytelling, this book focuses on the importance of the environment and of respecting the wisdom passed on by elders.

Emma's Gift
Deborah L. Delaronde (Métis)
Kegedonce 2014
Recommended for grades 2 to 5

A story about a young girl who learns the true meaning of her community's yearly King's Day Celebration, similar to Christmas, when her grandmother hurts her ankle.

Fatty Legs
Christy Jordan-Fenton and Margaret Pokiak-Fenton
Illustrated by Liz Amini-Holmes
Annick Press 2010
Recommended for ages 9 to12

A true story, written with Margaret Pokiak-Fenton's daughter-in-law, of the harsh awakening Margaret received when she attended residential school. Accompanied by archival photographs provided by Margaret, and illustrations.

Goodbye Buffalo Bay
Larry Loyie (Cree) with Constance Brissenden
Theytus Books 2008
Recommended for ages 8 to 11

Goodbye Buffalo Bay chronicles the life of Lawrence, a young teenage boy, during his final year at residential school, and his struggles afterward. The sequel to **As Long as the Rivers Flow** and **When the Spirits Dance Goodbye**.

Hiawatha and the Peacemaker
Robbie Robertson
Illustrated By David Shannon
Abrams Books 2015
Recommended for ages 4 to 8

The story of Hiawatha, the legendary historical figure who helped form the great Iroquois Nation.

I Am Not a Number
Jenny Kay Dupuis and Kathy Kacer
Illustrated by Gillian Newland
Second Story Press 2016
Recommended for ages 7 to 11

When Irene is taken from her First Nations family to a residential school, she is confused, frightened, and terribly homesick. When she goes home for the holidays, her parents decide never to send her away again, but what will happen when her parents disobey the law?

The Mishomis Book: The Voice of the Ojibway
Edward Benton-Banai
Illustrated by Joe Liles
Red School House 2010
Recommended for all ages

For people of all cultures, but especially for Ojibway and native youth, this is a detailed introduction to Ojibway culture and the sacred Midewiwin teachings, with its message that life should centre on respect for all living things.

Moonshot: The Indigenous Comics Collection, Vols. 1 & 2
Various Artists
Edited by Hope Nicholson
Alternate History Comics

A combination of traditional stories and futuristic tales involving Indigenous protagonists, created by a variety of Indigenous writers and artists from across North America.

No Time to Say Goodbye: Children's Stories of Kuper Island Residential School
Sylvia Olsen with Rita Morris and Ann Sam
Illustrated by Julia Bell and Connie Paul
Sono Nis Press 2001
Recommended for ages 8 and up

 Indigenous Peoples of Canada © Chalkboard Publishing Inc.

A fictionalized account of what happened when government agents took five children from the Tsartlip First Nation, a Coast Salish community in BC., to the isolated Kuper Island Residential School in the 1950s. Written in consultation with survivors of the school.

A Stranger at Home
Christy Jordan-Fenton and Margaret Pokiak-Fenton
Illustrated by Liz Amini-Holmes
Annick Press 2011
Recommended for ages 9 to12

The true story of Margaret, who, after two years at a residential school, finds on returning home to the high Arctic that she is now an outsider who can no longer speak her language or enjoy the food her mother makes for her. A sequel to **Fatty Legs**.

Secret Path
Gord Downie
Illustrated by Jeff Lemire
Simon & Schuster 2016
Recommended for ages 10 and up

This graphic novel, which was released in conjunction with an album of songs Downie wrote, tells the true tale of 12-year-old Chanie Wenjack, who lived at a residential school in northern Ontario, and what befell him when he ran away from the facility. With a companion animated film adapted from the book.

The Song Within My Heart
David Bouchard (Métis)
Illustrated by Allen Sap (Cree)
Raincoast Books 2002
Recommended for ages 6 and up

A story about a young Indigenous boy who is preparing for his first powwow with his Nokum (grandmother), who guides him through the day and watches over him as the day goes by.

When We Were Alone
David Alexander Robertson
Illustrated by Julie Flett (Cree-Métis)
HighWater Press 2016
Recommended for ages 4 to 8

A conversation between a young girl and her grandmother reveals what life was like for the older woman at the residential school she attended.

VIDEOS

Indigenous Art

The Art Show

Part of the CBC's series of videos for kids, several of these videos highlight Indigenous stories and crafts, with episodes such as Maci's Longhouse Painting, Joshua's White Pine, Kohen's Cornhusk Doll, etc.

https://www.bing.com/videos/search?q=Videos+for+kids+on+Aboriginal+culture+CBC&&view=-detail&mid=8FCEB94C73C8EB4969528FCEB94C73C8EB496952&&FORM=VRDGAR

Canadian Aboriginal Art

One in a series of YouTube videos for kids that highlight Indigenous culture and history.

https://www.bing.com/videos/search?q=Videos+for+kids+on+Aboriginal+-culture+and+history&&view=detail&mid=DC61E7B989158787A58EDC61E-7B989158787A58E&&FORM=VDRVRV

Indigenous Art for Kids

One in a series of YouTube videos for kids that highlight Indigenous culture and history.

https://www.bing.com/videos/search?q=Videos+for+kids+on+Aboriginal+cul-ture+and+history&&view=detail&mid=89EF8EB8C4987BA13B7889EF8EB8C-4987BA13B78&&FORM=VDRVRV

Indigenous History

Canadian Aboriginal History: Origins

One in a series of YouTube videos for kids that highlight Indigenous culture and history. Other videos in the series include First Nations in Canada; First Nations: A History; and The Legend of Weesakayjack: How North America Came to Be (animated), and many more.

https://www.bing.com/videos/search?q=Videos+for+kids+on+Aboriginal+cul-ture+and+history&&view=detail&mid=5D00E20E74B1CFBB60685D00E20E74B-1CFBB6068&&FORM=VRDGAR

Misconceptions about Aboriginal People

A YouTube video in which young Indigenous people address mistaken ideas people have about native people in the US.

https://www.bing.com/videos/search?q=Videos+for+kids+on+Aboriginal+culture+and+history&&view=detail&mid=119D97775A32997F6280119D97775A32997F6280&&FORM=VRDGAR

Indigenous Culture

Making Ceremonial Clothing

A step-by-step video that shows how to make a man's ceremonial bustle, used in Indigenous dance ceremonies and powwows.

https://www.bing.com/videos/search?q=Videos+of+Aboriginal+grammas+teaching+Grandchild+to+beadwork&&view=detail&mid=C5255579AB92F6E0915E-C5255579AB92F6E0915E&&FORM=VRDGAR

Throat Singing

One in a series of YouTube videos for kids that highlight Indigenous culture and history.

https://www.bing.com/videos/search?q=Videos+for+kids+on+Aboriginal+culture+and+history&&view=detail&mid=AD3B7544B3E1F3987C33AD3B7544B3E-1F3987C33&&FORM=VRDGAR

Baking Indian Bannock

A step-by-step video that shows how to make traditional bannock—the unleavened flour-and-water loaf also known as frybread—using common household ingredients.

https://www.bing.com/videos/search?q=Videos+for+kids+on+Aboriginal+baking+bannock&&view=detail&mid=E8F15D93123F391D4133E8F15D93123F391D4133&&FORM=VRD-GAR

I Am Anishinaabe

One in a series of YouTube videos for kids that highlight Indigenous culture and history.

https://www.bing.com/videos/search?q=Videos+for+kids+on+Aboriginal+culture+and+history&&view=detail&mid=BE5E1FB3871AFE4A90C5BE5E1FB3871AFE-4A90C5&&FORM=VDRVRV

TELEVISION / PODCASTS

Aboriginal Peoples Television Network

The Aboriginal Peoples Television Network (APTN) makes and airs programs made by, for, and about Indigenous peoples in Canada and the US. APTN Kids shows programs geared to children, and the website features games and activities you can download/print.

http://aptn.ca/kids/

I Am Indigenous

In separate videos, seven Indigenous community builders share their visions of empowering others to be proud of their past as they aim to create a brighter future.

http://www.cbc.ca/news2/interactives/i-am-indigenous-2017/

Unreserved—Podcasts

The CBC radio program features Indigenous storytellers, culture makers, and community shakers from across Canada, and a soundtrack showcasing the best in Indigenous music.

http://www.cbc.ca/radio/unreserved

Indigenous News

News stories from across the country, with a focus on those stories of particular interest to Canada's Indigenous communities.

http://www.cbc.ca/news/indigenous

NOTABLE INDIGENOUS PEOPLE

Elijah Harper (Ojibway-Cree)

The Canadian Press 1990 newsmaker of the year, Manitoba's lone Indigenous MLA is best known for the role he played in scuttling the Meech Lake Accord, which had been negotiated without consulting First Nations.

Alanis Obomsawin (Abenaki)

A singer, artist, and documentary filmmaker, Obomsawin addresses the struggles of Indigenous peoples in Canada. Her widely acclaimed documentary, *Kanehsatake: 270 Years of Resistance* (1993), deals with the 78-day Mohawk-government standoff at Oka, Quebec, in 1990.

Louis Riel (Métis)

Known as the Founding Father of Manitoba and a leader of the Métis, Riel fought to preserve the rights and culture of his people. Seen as a traitor by some and a hero by others, Riel, who was hanged in 1885, remains a controversial figure to this day.

Kenojuak Ashevak (Inuit)

An artist and printmaker, Kenojuak Ashevak is perhaps best known for her print *The Enchanted Owl*, which Canada Post featured on a stamp in 1970. She was also the first woman to become involved with the printmaking shop in Cape Dorset, Nunavut, an artistic co-operative with a worldwide reputation for producing high-quality, limited-edition Inuit prints.

Chief Dan George (Tsleil-Waututh)

Born in 1899 in British Columbia, Dan George was a poet, actor, and activist, and the first Indigenous person many people saw on TV and in the movies. He was nominated for an Academy Award for *Little Big Man.* Dan George spent much of his life trying to improve non-Indigenous people's understanding of Indigenous people.

Daphne Odjig (Odawa-Potawatomi)

A painter whose artistic career spanned six decades, Odjig is described as the driving force behind what was known as "the Indian Group of Seven." She brought her social awareness as a feminist Anishinaabe artist and activist to her art, creating a body of work that helped bring an Indigenous voice to the forefront of contemporary Canadian art.

Hiawatha (Mohawk or Onondaga)

The native leader is an important figure in the early history of present-day Ontario. Though many versions of his story exist, Hiawatha, who was born between the 12th and 13th centuries, is credited with persuading the Onondaga, Mohawk, Oneida, Cayuga, and Seneca tribes to unite and form the Iroquois confederacy of the Five Nations.

Rosemarie Kuptana (Inuit)

An Inuit rights activist, broadcaster, and journalist who was forced to attend a residential school as a child, Kuptana headed the Inuit Broadcasting Corporation, which, under her leadership, came to reflect and express Inuit culture and society. She also served for three terms as president of the Inuit Tapirisat of Canada, the national voice of 55,000 Inuit people.

Justice Murray Sinclair (Ojibway)

A lawyer, senator, and judge, Justice Sinclair is perhaps best known for presiding over Canada's Truth and Reconciliation Commission. In response to those who questioned why Indigenous people didn't just "get over" the trauma of residential schools, he said: "My answer has always been: Why can't you always remember this? Because this is about memorializing those people who have been the victims of a great wrong. Why don't you tell the United States to 'get over' 9/11?"

Mary Two-Axe Earley (Mohawk)

A human rights activist, elder, and advocate for women and children, Two-Axe Earley was a pioneer in the Canadian women's movement, successfully challenging Canadian laws, enshrined in the Indian Act, that discriminated against Indigenous women.

Michael Greyeyes (Plains Cree)

An actor, a former dancer with the National Ballet of Canada, a director, choreographer, and professor at York University in Ontario, Greyeyes has appeared on TV and in many feature films, including *Dance Me Outside, Passchendaele*, and *Smoke Signals*. The founding artistic director of Toronto's Signal Theatre, he was the subject of *He Who Dreams: Michael Greyeyes On The Powwow Trail*, a 1997 CBC documentary.

Buffy Sainte-Marie (Cree)

A singer-songwriter, composer, artist and activist, the multiple-award-winning Sainte-Marie has been an advocate for Indigenous issues in her music and her life. Artists as varied as Elvis Presley and Neko Case have covered her songs, including *Universal Soldier* and *Until It's Time For You To Go*. She is an Officer of the Order of Canada, and has been inducted into the Canadian Music Hall of Fame, the Canadian Country Music Hall of Fame, and Canada's Walk of Fame, among many honours.

Alex Janvier (Dene-Salteaux)

Janvier, a painter, is often referred to as the first Indigenous Canadian modern artist. Janvier was born in 1935 on the LeGoff Reserve of the Cold Lake First Nation in Alberta. At the age of eight, he was taken from his family to a residential school in northern Alberta, where he made his first paintings. He studied at the Alberta College of Art and Design and graduated in 1960. Many of his paintings focus on the traditional bead and quillwork of the Dene First Nation.

Map of Canada

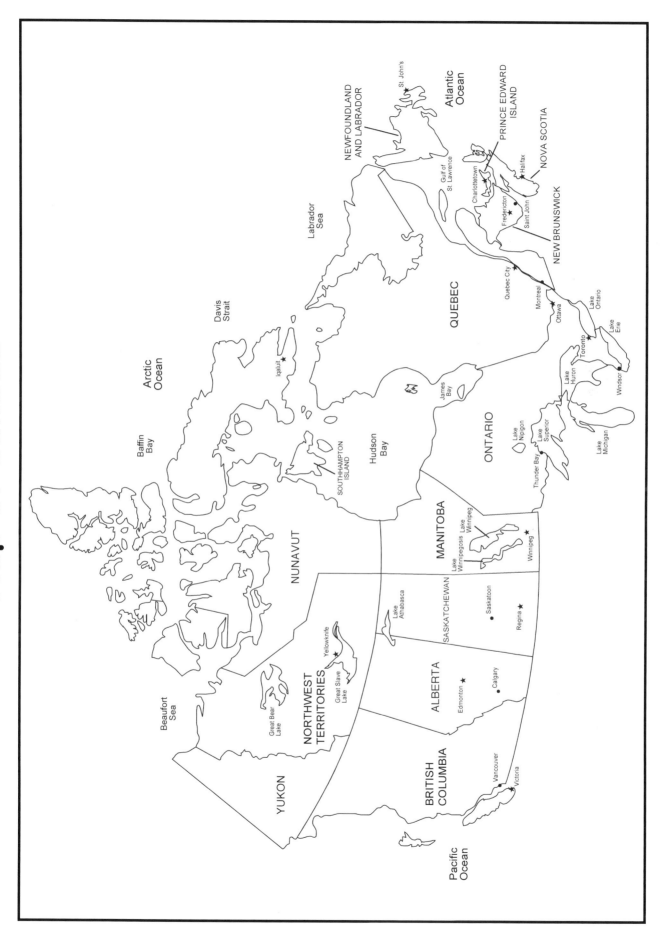

Answers to Exercises

Turtle Island, p. 5

1. The Creator decided to purify the Earth by causing a huge flood to cover it.
2. The animals planned to use the earth to make new land where they could raise their families.
3. They all knew the loon was a good diver.
4. The muskrat had a little ball of earth in his paw.
5. The turtle offered his strong back to hold up the piece of earth. The wind blew on it until there was a huge island in the midst of all the waters.
6. Answers will vary.
7. Answers will vary.

Peoples of the Northwest Coast, p. 7

1. Ensure three of the following are chosen: Coast Salish, Gitxsan, Haida, Nisga'a, Nuuchah-nulth (Nootka), or Tlingit.
2. They lived in an area full of trees for building that also provided fish and other animals to eat.
3. They ate some or all of the following: clams, crabs, oysters; bears, deer, water birds, whales; berries, camas (wild hyacinth) bulbs, ferns, and seaweed.
4. A *mortuary pole* was a totem pole with a grave box at the top.
5. Black represents power; white represents the heavens; blue represents the sky and water; red represents war.
6. Cedar trees provided wood for houses and canoes; cedar branches were braided into fishing lines, nets, and ropes; and cedar bark was woven into clothing or hats.

Peoples of the Plateau, p. 9

1. The Peoples of the Plateau lived in what is today British Columbia, between the Coast Mountains and the Rocky Mountains.
2. Pit houses looked like large domes covered with earth and tree boughs. A notched log stuck out the top to help people climb in and out.
3. They harpooned fish, dipped fishing nets into the water, speared fish and trapped fish in woven baskets.
4. In winter, they travelled using toboggans and snowshoes.
5. Sturgeon-nosed canoes had pointed tips that sat just above the waterline. The unique shape helped keep water out of the canoe.
6. The Stl'atl'imx peoples are still known for the baskets they make from cedar tree roots.

Peoples of the Plains, p. 11

1. They travelled across what is now Alberta, Saskatchewan, and much of Manitoba.
2. They moved around following the herds of buffalo.
3. Assiniboine = Nakoda; Kainai = Blood; Nehiyauak = Plains Cree; Pikuni = Peigan; Siksika = Blackfoot
4. A *travois* is a frame made by fastening two pine poles together in a V-shape. It is pulled by a dog or horse.
5. Buffalo hides were used to make clothing; bones were used for tools; tendons were used as thread; horns were used as cups; and tails were used as whisks.
6. Porcupine quillwork adorned animal-skin bags, clothing, and moccasins.

Peoples of the Arctic, p. 13

1. Northern Quebec, northern Labrador, the Northwest Territories and Yukon, and Nunavut make up the Inuit Nunangat.
2. They moved three or four times a year, with the seasons, usually to hunt.
3. They caught caribou, musk oxen, Arctic hare, polar bear, seal, whale, walrus, duck, fox and wolf. They fished for Arctic char, salmon, trout, and whitefish.
4. *Mukluks* are watertight boots. The word comes from an Indigenous word, "maklak," which means "bearded seal."
5. Inuit myths and legends told how the sun, moon, and stars came into being, and explained the existence of good and evil.
6. The Inuit believed that Sedna controlled many animals who lived in the sea, and that they must keep Sedna happy so she would let them continue to hunt them.

Peoples of the Subarctic, p. 19

1. They lived in an area that stretched over most of northern Canada, from Yukon to Newfoundland.
2. The Gwich'in (Kutchin), Innu, Montagnais, Naskapi, and Yellowknife nations lived there.
3. They lived in tipis, wigwams, lean-tos, and ridgepole lodges.
4. A *tumpline* was a piece of cloth or animal hide that a hunter fastened around a load, then around his forehead to support the weight of the pack.
5. Women set snares, preserved meat, cleaned hides, fished, and picked berries, dandelions, moss, and other plants.
6. Children were taught how important it is to have good relations with the spirits of animals and with nature, since it was believed these could affect people's well-being.

Farmers of the Eastern Woodlands, p. 21

1. The lived on the shores of both Ontario's Great Lakes and the St. Lawrence River in Ontario.
2. Iroquois = Haudenosaunee; Petun = Tionontati; Huron = Wendat
3. Palisades were rows of posts with sharp points. There could be as many as three rows around a single village.
4. They lived in longhouses, which were long, rectangular buildings with rounded roofs.
5. The Three Sisters were corn, beans and squash. The Corn was righteous and stood tall and straight; the shy Bean clutched the Corn's legs, and the Squash, spreading about on the ground, was the troublemaker.
6. Corn was a very important crop because it could be dried and made into soup to feed a village throughout the winter.

Hunters of the Eastern Woodlands, p. 24

1. They survived by fishing and gathering wild plants.
2. They were known as Algonquians.
3. First Nations who lived by lakes or swamps harvested wild rice.
4. They used birchbark to create canoes, wigwams, and baskets; to wrap and store food; to help stop a wound from bleeding; and, when rolled into a cone, to make a moose call.
5. A tea made from cedar bark provided vitamin C, and willow tree bark had a pain-killing drug in it.
6. Pelts are animal skins that still have fur on them; hides are skins with no fur.

Names of Indigenous Peoples, p. 26

1. The Ojibway people got their name from a word meaning "puckered," which refers to the puckered moccasins they wore.
2. Sample answers: Indigenous peoples might have more than one name because they may have changed their names over the years, or because English, French, and other European settlers were often unable to pronounce some Indigenous names, so they created other names.
3. If someone calls you a snake, they might be suggesting you are sneaky or untrustworthy.
4. The Blackfoot got their name from their dark moccasins. The Huron people got their name from the French because of their hairstyle. The Haudenosaunee name refers to the style of house in which they lived. The Ojibway got their name from the style of moccasins they wore.
5. The Nass River was important to the Nisga'a people because there were a lot of fish in the river and they depended on it for food.
6. Answers will vary.

Who are the Wendat? p. 29

1. The name Wendat means "people who live on the back of a great turtle."
2. A Wendat village was usually located on a hill that had a marsh or swamp around the bottom, which made the village easy to defend.
3. Some longhouses could fit more than ten families.
4. To make a field ready to plant, the Wendat burned the trees and grass where they wanted to plant. The ash from the fire fertilized the soil.
5. Every 10 to 15 years, the crops would use up the nutrients in the soil and all the nearby firewood would have been cut down.
6. Huron means "wild boar." The French gave the Wendat this nickname because the Indigenous men's bristly hairstyle reminded them of the wild animal.

The League of Six Nations, p. 31

1. The Cayuga, Mohawk, Oneida, Onondaga, Seneca, and, later, the Tuscarora
2. *Sachem* means chief. The sachem spoke for the family.
3. The spreading roots of the pine tree represent how any person looking for peace can follow the roots and find the shelter of the great peace.
4. Deganawideh and Hiawatha were able to bring the five nations together to form a league.
5. The Great Law of Peace sees people as being members of one family, which has just one body, one heart, and one mind.
6. Canada's largest First Nations reserve is near Brantford, in southwestern Ontario.

The Métis, p. 33

1. The Métis live mostly in Alberta, Saskatchewan, Manitoba, and Ontario.
2. They depended on the Métis to guide them through the Canadian wilderness, help them live in the woods, and supply them with pemmican.
3. *Ceinture fléchée* means "arrowed sash." It was important because it could be used to carry rope and saddle blankets, among other things.
4. In 1868, Louis Riel and his followers moved in to stop Canadian officials from entering the Métis Red River Settlement.
5. In 1869, Canada recognized Métis rights and created the province of Manitoba, with Riel as its leader.
6. Answers will vary.

Indigenous Culture, p. 35

1. There are many ways to learn about Indigenous culture: from artifacts, pictures, pictographs, petroglyphs, legends, and stories.

2. *Pictographs* are painted pictures and *petroglyphs* are images carved into rock.
3. It is important to pass along Indigenous legends because they draw the Indigenous peoples together, keep history and culture alive, pass along information, and give ideas for coping with similar situations.
4. Archeological digs can tell scientists where and how Indigenous peoples lived, what was important to them, how they built their homes, what materials they used, what clothes they wore, and more.
5. *Wampum belts* are made of shell beads strung together, and were made to record treaties or historic events. The shell beads could also be used as money.
6. Answers will vary. Ensure the words and images match.

Indigenous Communities, p. 38
1. Indigenous communities were organized along family lines. Sample answer: I think it was a good way to organize communities because everyone got a say in what happened, they were more likely to come to an agreement, everyone's needs would be heard and taken care of.
2. Indigenous elders hold the knowledge and pass it along, they advise leaders, teach children about their responsibilities, teach respect for creation and the gifts of the Creator, and more.
3. Indigenous girls learned how to cook food, prepare animal skins, and sew clothing.
4. Indigenous boys learned how to fish and hunt successfully.
5. A *talking circle* is a way some Indigenous peoples make decisions. It involves everyone having a chance to talk with everyone equally, with no leader or followers.
6.

Responsibilities of Indigenous Men	Both	Responsibilities of Indigenous Women
• hunting large animals • building homes • trading with other Indigenous groups • fighting other First Nations when necessary • clearing the land for planting	• caring for children • teaching children skills • feeding the community • listening to elders	• hunting small animals and birds • gathering food • planting and harvesting crops • cooking • drying and scraping animal skins to make clothing

Tipis, Longhouses, and Igloos, p. 41
1. The Nehiyawak (Plains Cree), Pikuni (Peigan) and Siksika (Blackfoot) built tipis.
2. Tipis were easy to transport and could be set up quickly, and the people of the Plains travelled a lot, so needed homes that were portable.
3. The Ktunaxa, Secwepemc, and Stl'atl'imx lived in pit houses in the winter.
4. The Inuit had to use snow because In the Arctic there are no trees to supply wood.
5. Possible answer: So they could face the water and keep watch for enemies approaching.
6. Longhouses built in central Canada featured rounded roofs that were covered with elm, ash, or fir bark.

Getting Around—Transportation, p. 44
1. Cedar and birch trees were used to make canoes.
2. Umiak means "open-skinned boat."
3. A kayak was so light that a man could carry it over his head. This meant he could walk over ice to open water to hunt or fish.
4. They didn't have horses to ride or carry their belongings until the 1700s.
5. They used snowshoes, toboggans, and sleds (OR dog sleds).
6. Nails or pins weren't used in sleds because the bumpy, frozen ground would have knocked them out. Animal hide was used to lash the sled pieces together.

The Women of the Haudenosaunee Confederacy, p. 47
1. The Haudenosaunee Confederacy was formed by a group of nations so they could live in peace. So it was an agreement among groups for the purpose of living in peace.
2. The Grand Council dealt with matters that affected all the nations in the confederacy. So each nation's council dealt with matters that affected only their nation.
3. *Matrilineal* comes from words that mean "mother" and "a direct line." In the Haudenosaunee Confederacy, the clan people belonged to was passed down in a direct line from the mother to the child.
4. The Great Law of Peace provided a way to settle differences by thinking and negotiating rather than violence and warfare. This would stop the nations from fighting with each other so people would not be killed. They could spend more time making their lives better.
5. The five nations were the Mohawk, Oneida, Onondaga, Cayuga, and Seneca.

Indigenous People and the Environment, p. 49

1. Answers will vary. Sample answer: Today, people buy building supplies, food, and clothing at a store. They get medicine from a doctor or a pharmacy.
2. Foods Indigenous people hunted include animals such as moose, deer, buffalo, and rabbit; they caught fish; and they gathered the eggs of wild birds, berries, nuts, fruit, mushrooms, wild rice, herbs, and edible roots.
3. Indigenous people used wood and bark in houses, sleds, canoes, and snowshoes.
4. Indigenous people showed respect for animals they caught by using every part of them.
5. Answers may vary.

Indigenous Inventions, p. 51

1. A kayak is narrow and pointed at both ends. This could help it to move through waterways that might be partly blocked by ice. The paddle used with a kayak has a blade on each end. That means a person can paddle a kayak alone and can paddle through narrow passageways. A person using a two-sided paddle can generate speed without moving his or her body much. This is helpful because the person is probably wearing lots of clothes to stay warm, and it is hard to move when you are wearing a lot of layers.
2. You can make syrup by boiling the sap, and you can make maple candy by pouring the boiled syrup into the snow.
3. Sample answer: I think it is important to be able to get around quickly and easily so that we are not too tired to do the job we need to do when we get to where we need to be. Getting around quickly also means that jobs take less time to do, giving us more time to spend with our friends and families.
4. Sample answer: Vitamin C is a vitamin that is found in many fruits and vegetables. I get my vitamin C by drinking orange juice in the morning before school. I think it was important for Indigenous people to find other ways to get vitamin C because they did not have fruits and vegetables in the winter when it snowed and they could not get fruits and vegetables from far away the way we can. People need vitamin C to stay healthy.

The First Visitors to Turtle Island, p. 53

1. The first explorers came to Turtle Island from Scandinavia about 1,000 years ago.
2. The settlement was called L'Anse aux Meadows.
3. The Beothuk showed them where to fish; how to hunt; which plants could be eaten and which used for medicine; how to build homes; and how to dry and prepare animals skins.
4. They received weapons, food, and iron tools, such as axes.

5. a) The Beothuk made treaties simply by shaking hands. b) Answers will vary.
6. In 1960, the site of the Viking settlement was rediscovered.

Why Explorers Came to Canada, p. 55

1. Explorers set out to discover if they could sail to China. They had no idea that an entire continent lay between them and Asia. In fact, when early explorers first came to North America, they thought they had reached China.
2. The Silk Road over the lands through Europe and Asia was very long, and bandits and robbers made it very dangerous. Traders wondered if there was a different way to reach China.
3. Most European countries competed with each other for wealth and power.
4. A *missionary* is a person who spreads their religion to other people and places.
5. Answers will vary. Sample answer: The fish would rot on a boat all the way back to Europe because they did not have refrigeration. Dried fish would have lasted longer.
6. Answers will vary. Sample answer: It would be very scary to travel without a map. I think I would feel afraid, but also very brave because not very many people would have the courage to explore new places.

The Fur Trade, p. 57

1. Furs that they traded for with the Indigenous people caused them explore the country.
2. The Indigenous people wanted the fishermen's metal tools, including knives and axes, since they were much sharper than the stone tools they used.
3. The most popular fur was beaver.
4. The fishermen knew they could make a lot of money from beaver fur in Europe, where it was used to make hats.
5. In 1670 the Hudson's Bay Company was set up for the fur trade.
6. Voyageurs were French Canadians who transported furs by canoe. *Voyageur* is French for "traveller."

Fur Trade Routes, p. 59

1. The St. Lawrence River was connected to many other smaller rivers, which allowed the Europeans to explore what is now Ontario and Quebec.
2. The fur traders travelled through the Great Lakes to the far end of Lake Superior, which allowed them to begin exploring the Prairies.
3. They trekked along mountain passes through the Rocky Mountains and along the Columbia River to the Pacific Ocean.

4. *Portage* means to carry a boat or goods on land between two bodies of water.
5. Rapids and waterfalls couldn't be paddled through, so the traders had to portage.
6. Simon Fraser is an explorer who in 1808 travelled through BC and the waterway now known as the Fraser River.

Peace and Friendship Treaties, p. 61
1. The treaties helped them to work out boundaries of territories, to trade goods, and to travel safely through the territories of other Indigenous groups.
2. They gave them beads, mirrors, and tobacco in exchange for beaver skins.
3. During the 1600s and 1700s, Britain and France fought each other for control of what is now Canada.
4. The treaty recognized that Maliseet and Mi'kmaq owned the land, and it included rules for the relationship between the Indigenous peoples and the British.
5. Peace and Friendship Treaties differ from other treaties in that they don't involve an exchange of land, hunting rights, payments, or other benefits.

Samuel de Champlain, p. 64
1. Starting in the 1500s, explorers came to North America and claimed land for their countries. These countries were France, Britain, and Spain. The map shows that in the 1600s, France had most of the land in eastern North America. New France included land from around the Great Lakes all the way down to Louisiana. Britain claimed land along the coast. This was the Thirteen Colonies. They also claimed land above New France and around Hudson's Bay. This was called Rupert's Land. Spain claimed land in the south. There was a lot of land that was not claimed by anyone.
2. In 1608, Champlain founded a colony that became Quebec City. He formed an alliance with the Huron and Algonquin against their enemy, the Iroquois. He discovered and named Lake Champlain. In July, Champlain and his First Nations allies won a battle against the Iroquois, and the Iroquois became enemies of the French.
3. *Alliance* and *allies* have the same root word. An alliance is a thing or idea. Champlain formed an alliance with the Huron and Algonquin. Allies are people. Champlain's allies were the Indigenous peoples.

4. Champlain formed an alliance with the Huron and Algonquin. The Iroquois were enemies of the Huron and Algonquin. Champlain fought against the Iroquois to help the Huron and Algonquin. So the Iroquois became the enemies of the French too.
5. Champlain explored and mapped much of New France, including the St. Lawrence River and the Atlantic coast. Champlain founded colonies such as Saint Croix Island, Port Royal, and Quebec City. From 1620 on, he governed New France, except when he was a prisoner in England.

Fur Traders and Settlers in New France, p. 67
1. Fur traders came to get furs. Settlers came to farm. Differences: Fur traders spent most of their time trading for furs with the First Nations. They explored new land looking for furs. Settlers lived in permanent settlements. They spent most of their time growing crops.
2. Sample answer: I learned that the women were single, and some were orphaned. They were chosen because the single women were looking for husbands, and the orphaned women did not have families that would not want them to go. They had to be single so they could get married in New France.
3. Some settlers worked in the fur trade to get more money because they would not make a lot of money from farming. They had to build their farms and pay taxes so they probably did not have a lot of money to buy other things that they needed.
4. The fur traders got their furs from the First Nations. They traded things with the First Nations for the furs. The First Nations hunted to get furs to trade. Some fur traders married First Nations women.
5. Before, they would only hunt for what they needed. Then they started hunting animals for their fur only. Some animals became endangered. Also, many fur traders married First Nations women. Their children became the first Métis.

Indigenous Women and the Fur Trade, p. 69

1.

Knowledge of the Land	• acted as guides and interpreters • knew the cultures of various First Nations, and many of the languages • could guide Europeans through the wilderness trails and along rivers and lakes • knew the best places for setting up and preparing campsites • gathered firewood and made fires • cooked meals • made comfortable beds out of tree boughs and furs
Food for Survival	• cooked meals • knew which leaves, roots, shoots, and berries could be eaten • knew how to fish and how to trap animals for food • knew how to preserve food so that it could be eaten throughout the winters, when fresh food was hard to find • dried berries and other fruits in the sun or over a fire • ground corn into meal that they could store and use for making bread when needed
Preparing Furs	• knew how to clean and prepare furs so they could be sent to Europe, where they would be sold for high prices • knew where to find the animals with the best skins • knew how to trap the animals • knew how to scrape, stretch, and dry the skins

2. Besides acting as interpreters, Indigenous women knew the land and water routes, where to find the animals with the best fur, and how to trap, skin, dry, and prepare them for sale in Europe. They knew the best campsites and how to set them up. They also knew which plants, animals, and fish to eat, where to find them, and how to prepare them for eating.

3. It was important that the Indigenous women knew how to preserve food because it kept them and the Europeans fed through the winter when fresh food was hard to find.

4. a) pemmican: a mixture of dried meat, fat, and berries b) sagamit: corn stew c) bannock: a flatbread

5. Indigenous women ground corn into meal that they could store and use for making bread when needed.

Explorers Depended on Indigenous People, p. 71

1. Students should list any two of the following examples from each category:

Eating well and staying healthy	• teaching them which berries, roots, and fruit were safe to eat • showing them how to trap animals for food and fur • sharing medicines made from the plants around them • teaching them how to make foods such as pemmican and bannock which, were long-lasting, easy to carry while travelling, and highly nutritious
Getting around	• sharing their knowledge of the land • guiding them and showing them the best land and water routes • making maps of travel routes • sharing inventions such as snowshoes, sleds, and birchbark canoes
Surviving the cold	• teaching them how to survive the winter by making tea from cedar bark and leaves to prevent scurvy • making them fur coats, leggings, and mittens from animal furs and skins

2. You might wish to have students share their letters with the class.
3. *Scurvy* is a disease caused by a lack of vitamin C. First Nations taught the Europeans how to make a tea from cedar bark and leaves. The tea was full of vitamin C and helped save the settlers' lives.
4. Indigenous women sewed fur coats, leggings, and mittens for the Europeans.

The Indian Act, p. 73

1. The Indian Act sets out how the government works with the country's more than 600 First Nations.
2. To decide who could have "Indian" status; to absorb First Nations into Canadian society; and to set out which land First Nations could use
3. The Indian Act applies only to First Nations, not to the Métis or Inuit.
4. A *potlatch* is a gift-giving ceremony which is very important to west coast First Nations for building connections in the community.
5. The Indian Act causes problems today because the Canadian government passed it without any input or agreement from First Nations.

6. The change means people who don't have Indigenous status can finally live on First Nations reserves with their families. Sample answer: This change would be important because all members of a family could live together on a reserve, and pass on their culture and traditions.

First Nations Reserves, p. 75
1. A *reserve* is land that has been set apart by the government for a First Nations band to use.
2. Many reserves are in remote countryside, which means few businesses or jobs. Health and education services may be limited, and many reserves have water that is not safe to drink.
3. The Six Nations of the Grand River and the Mohawks of Akwesasne reserves in Ontario have the largest populations.
4. First Nations were able to create urban reserves thanks to land claim settlements.
5. The Fishing Lake First Nations set up the first urban reserve in 1981 at Kylemore in Saskatchewan.
6. First Nations University of Canada is Canada's first university on a reserve. It is in Regina.

Residential Schools, p. 77
1. Residential schools were set up to force Indigenous people to assimilate into the culture of Canada's settlers.
2. The Canadian government believed that if Indigenous children were schooled by non-Indigenous teachers, they would forget about their customs, families, language, and Indigenous past.
3. Answers may vary. Ensure the child chooses two of the following: their long hair was cut; their names were changed; they were punished, sometimes beaten, for speaking their Indigenous languages; they were abused mentally, physically, and sexually; they were rarely allowed to visit their families.
4. The children were very damaged and found it difficult to fit into the traditional cultures of their communities. They did not know how to be parents because they had grown up without any, being cared for by strangers.
5. It was set up to look into the abuse caused by the residential schools.
6. Sample answers: Indigenous people probably feel angry, confused, wronged, and hurt. They probably feel the schools were very unjust and cruel, and should never have been allowed to do what they did to Indigenous families. They probably feel that they were robbed of their childhood and culture, and that they deserve an apology.

Land Claims, p. 79
1. The government signed treaties with First Nations to allow settlers to create settlements on First Nations land.
2. These treaties outlined how the two groups would live on the land.
3. The government didn't always give First Nations all the land the treaties promised, so the First Nations had to negotiate with the Canadian government either to get back their original land or to receive land somewhere else.
4. "Comprehensive claims" are called modern treaties because they are about First Nations land rights that haven't been covered in historic treaties.
5. The Osoyoos band in BC, the Peguis First Nation in Manitoba, and the Chapleau Cree First Nation in Ontario successfully negotiated land claim settlements.
6. Nunavut was created because many Inuit wanted land where they could make decisions for themselves.

What is a Powwow? p. 81
1. Indigenous people come together to celebrate their traditions through singing, dancing, eating, and the selling of handmade arts and crafts.
2. A powwow always has dancing, drumming, and singing.
3. *Regalia* are elaborate clothing, specially made moccasins, fans, headdresses, and jewellery.
4. Singing, dancing, drumming, and regalia are sacred elements of a powwow.
5. There are two main types of powwows: competitive and traditional. At competitive powwows, dancers and musicians compete for prizes.
6. Answers will vary.

Indigenous Symbols Today, p. 83
1. The colours are blue, white, red, and yellow. They symbolize Nunavut's wealth.
2. The sun, grass, and water on the Treaty 6 medal symbolize the treaty's endurance for "as long as the sun shines, the grass grows and the water flows."
3. An *infinity symbol* looks like a figure eight on its side. It represents the Indigenous and European peoples that came together to make one unique culture, the Métis.
4. Orange Shirt Day is on September 30 each year. It reminds people of the many First Nations children who were forced to attend residential schools.
5. An Inukshuk pointed the way, showed where someone had gone so that others could follow, or marked a place where food was hidden.